KU-486-783

CONTENTS

Introduction

I T has always seemed to me that 'Question Time' in the House of Commons is a splendid idea. When so much parliamentary time has to be taken up with making and hearing speeches, members are given this daily opportunity of seeking direct information from the ministers of state. It may be that the government spokesmen have to admit ignorance, or that their answers fail to satisfy the questioner; but there can be no deliberate evasion of the issue.

So often in the middle of a talk or sermon thoughts and questions arise in our minds, but we cannot interrupt the speaker's flow to ask for an explanation of what he is saying. That is why, when the opportunity arises, I always like to give people the chance to ask questions about the Christian life. Again and again, either singly or as a member of some sort of panel, I have tried to deal with the questions to which people want answers, and quite apart from any help I have been able to give, I have always found it a most stimulating experience.

That is really why this book came to be written. It tries to deal with a number of doctrinal questions nearly all of which have been put to me at one time or another in some shape or form, and which I find other people are being asked as well.

I hope no one will run away with the idea that I know all the answers. Nothing could be farther from the truth. What I have tried to do is to explain what Scripture itself teaches on any given subject, and it will be to the reader's advantage to follow up each answer by studying the Bible carefully with the aid of a Concordance. He will find that this has been made easier by the fact that, except where otherwise stated, all quotations are from the Authorized Version. In cases where there is no specifically scriptural answer to a question, I have sought to give the one most generally accepted by Christians.

It is my chief hope in writing the book that it will help people into a clearer understanding of the true meaning of the Christian faith, and equip them to explain it more effectively to others.

Crowborough, February, 1966   John Eddison

1 | Is there sufficient evidence for believing in the existence of God ?

I READ recently that the best answer to an atheist is to give him a good dinner, and then to ask him if he believes there is a cook. It is not a bad idea, but probably any of us who have talked with atheists have not found it quite as simple as that. They have asked, as it were, to be taken into the kitchen, and to be furnished with a final and scientific proof of God's existence; and that we cannot do. But while there may be no way of proving that there is a God, the evidence we can accumulate makes it perfectly reasonable for an intelligent person to believe in Him.

Let us start by examining the *universe*. Perhaps the most striking thing we observe is the consistency of its laws—physical, chemical and biological, such as the law of gravity, for example—which extends to the utmost limits of our knowledge. This consistency shows itself in the order we see all around us, and also in the way in which very simple structures are repeated and combined to form complex ones in a definite pattern and unity; and it can be satisfactorily explained from a scientific point of view only if we accept the fact that it is derived from a single source.

When we turn from the universe to *ourselves*, it seems reasonable and indeed necessary to assume that this source must be at least as complex in its nature and structure as we are ourselves. That is to say, our natures, personalities and intuitions of right and wrong all require a satisfactory explanation, and this can only be found in the existence of an intelligent, personal and moral source and sustainer.

Further, a study of *anthropology* confirms that there is in man a universal sense of dependence upon a supremely high God, creator of 'the ends of the earth', and sustainer of all things. Of course, this instinct for God often expresses itself in crude and primitive ways, but its very

presence is of great significance. The Germans call it
Gottbetrunken, or *God-thirst*, and it seems inconceivable
that man should have been made in such a way that he can
only find his ultimate hope and satisfaction by trying to
believe in something which does not exist.

From anthropology, let us turn to *history*. We cannot
lightly dismiss the millions of people who claim that their
experience of God has been the most vivid and powerful
influence in their lives. In the Bible alone, for example, we
read of countless men and women who claim to have enjoyed intimate fellowship with Him, and to have experienced His help. Such people have found in Him not only
the chief integrating force in their own personal lives, but
also the only really satisfying answer to the problems of the
world in which they live.

This leads us finally to consider the intervention of one
Person, *Jesus Christ*, Who claimed to be the human em-
bodiment of God, and Whose character, teaching and work
supported those claims in a unique and overwhelming way.
Moreover, what He revealed to us confirms the idea of God
which we have already based upon our previous observa-
tions of the universe and of man. If the claims which Jesus
made are valid, then we can confidently say that He pro-
vides us with the crowning piece of evidence which we need
to believe in the existence of a God Who may be known
and loved. Archbishop William Temple sums it up for us
when he says, "If the gospel is true, and God is as the Bible
declares, a living God, the ultimate truth is not a system of
propositions, grasped by a perfect intelligence, but a personal being, apprehended by love."

These arguments do not add up to a positive and irrefut-
able proof for the existence of God. That would be too
much to expect, because conclusive proof of His existence
would require something greater than God to which we
could refer Him, and that in the nature of things is impossible. But they do show that belief in Him is not a blind
leap in the dark, nor a hazardous gamble against heavily
weighted odds, but rather a thoroughly sensible attitude of

mind for any rational and intelligent person to adopt. In fact, I would go further and say that the thoughtful, humble and unprejudiced mind should find itself carried by this collective evidence 'beyond all reasonable doubt', and the burden of proof on the other side—"Is there sufficient evidence for believing that there is no God?"

2 | If there is a God, where did He come from and where does He live?

IN one form or another this question has often been put to me. In the mind of the person asking it, to assume the existence of God introduces further problems. If there is a God, then who made Him? And if there is a God, where precisely does He live, within space and time or outside it?

The problems really arise because we human beings can only think sensibly in terms of space and time. To us everything must have a beginning and an ending, and every event must come before or after something else. But when the Bible speaks about God, and when it starts by saying, "In the beginning God . . .", it is really trying to tell us that Someone exists to Whom these human terms cannot be applied. In other words, God is 'uncaused', and Himself the cause of everything there is. Again, when we discuss His place of residence, we are told that He lives in 'heaven' or that He "inhabiteth eternity", which is just another way of saying that He belongs to a world of reality about which we can know practically nothing at all.

Perhaps it is felt that these answers are very unsatisfactory and inadequate. That may be so. The problem, however, is not so much that there is no answer, but rather that we would not be able to understand the answer if it were given, because we lack the necessary mental and spiritual equipment to do so; and when one day we are furnished with the right sort of apparatus, then we shall find that we no longer need to ask the questions!

Perhaps therefore it would be a good idea to take this opportunity of trying to see why we cannot fully understand the answers to questions of this sort. An analogy may help. Imagine two dogs talking together in their kennel after they have been shut up for the night. They are discussing their owner, their 'god', the man who looks after them, and without whom their lives would have little meaning or purpose. They discuss where he is, what he is doing, where he came from; but immediately they find themselves out of their depth, because they realize that he lives in a completely different world from theirs. They inhabit the kennel, the house and the garden, and parts of the countryside; but he, from their point of view, inhabits eternity, enjoying a family, social and business life of which they can know next to nothing.

Of course, the two worlds often intersect. Every day he takes them for a walk, and talks to them as if they were his friends. But even so, they realize that they represent only one tiny area of his existence, and when he has left them, he returns to a life which functions on a completely different plane, and which, from their limited, canine point of view seems to have neither beginning nor ending. Although they delight in their master's company, and depend upon him, they are not mentally equipped to think in human terms or to discuss human problems.

That is a picture of the position in which we find ourselves with regard to God. We have got to get used to the fact that there is more than one field or plane of reality. Of course, there are frequent occasions on which those two planes intersect. The supreme instance was when Jesus Christ 'invaded' our world of space and time and matter, rather as if the dog-owner were to leave his comfortable house and go and live in the kennel.

But even when they do intersect, our understanding is limited by very narrow horizons. We are rather like people living on 'flatland', or a piece of paper. We can understand length and breadth all right, but any idea of height or depth simply doesn't make sense. If a three-dimensional object, such as an orange, passes through our flat, two-dimensional world, we are only aware of a series of rings getting larger and larger, and then smaller and smaller, until they finally disappear altogether. Our minds cannot grasp the idea of a 'sphere' or 'volume' any more than the human mind can get to grips with such terms as 'eternity' and 'infinity'. We are like people in a foreign country who do not know the language or have the right currency.

It is, in fact, as impossible for us to think coherently about a God Who never began to exist and will never cease to do so as it is for those dogs to think sensibly and rationally about the man to whom they belong. Or, to change the metaphor, we are rather like the characters in a book who are trying to puzzle out how it is that they can live for twenty years, or travel thousands of miles, while their author or creator barely has time to drink a cup of tea.

3 | Is there any purpose in man's existence ?

A swiss girl once wanted to ask a friend of mine the question, "What on earth are you doing?" But her English was very imperfect, and she got it the wrong way round, and said, "What are you doing on earth?" It is a very good question, and one which everyone ought to ask himself. Why am I here? What is the point of my existence?

One of the troubles of the last hundred years is that science has focussed our attention almost exclusively on man's past. Ever since Darwin, people have been asking 'Where has man come from?' 'How did he get here?' These questions are important, it is true; but even more vital than the matter of our origin is that of our destiny—'Why am I here?' 'Where am I going?'

We can often tell what an object has been made for, and understand its purpose, by studying its nature, form and shape. A chair, for example, has pretty obviously been made to be sat upon and a tumbler to be drunk out of. Now in the same sort of way there are certain characteristics about man which give us a shrewd idea of the reason for his existence. There are, for example, his self-awareness, his sense of moral responsibility to a supreme Being outside himself, his sense of a need for forgiveness, his desire for friendship, and his awareness (at certain times more than others) of the spiritual world and the life after death. All these things taken together seem to suggest that man has not been created simply to enjoy an animal-like existence, but for some much higher and better purpose altogether.

We may, I think, go further, and say that man belongs to that class of object which has meaning or sense only if it is related to something else. Thus a record is a useless thing unless you have a record-player. Its purpose in life depends upon its relationship to something else. Man has been made for God, and when this relationship comes into existence, then everything fits into place, and the purpose of his reason, conscience and spirit becomes apparent.

It was St. Augustine who said, "O God, Thou hast made us for Thyself, and our hearts are restless until they find repose in Thee." In other words, we are made in such a way that we can only find true happiness and satisfaction in a personal relationship with God. The reason why there is so much restlessness and dis-ease in the world is simply that man who was made to live for God is trying to remove the Maker's name from his life and to do without Him; and is seeking in money, adventure, pleasure and a hundred other places for the contentment and self-fulfilment he craves.

So far we have looked at this question entirely from man's point of view, and deduced from the way in which we are made that we need God if we are to fulfil our real purpose in life. But we must also look at it from the point of view of God Himself. Can it be said that He wants us?

Is there any sense in which He would be less satisfied or in some way disappointed if man did not exist?

I think there is. The Bible reveals God to us in two principal ways—as a Creator and as a Father. Just as the artist must paint, and the musician must compose, so God must create. And He does so, the Bible tells us, for two reasons: first for His pleasure, and secondly for His glory. The creation of man was God's masterpiece, and when it was finished "it was very good"; and just as the painter enjoys his picture, so God hoped to derive infinite pleasure from the companionship and worship of man. We were also made to glorify Him by reflecting His power and goodness throughout the world. We know that God must have been bitterly disappointed when His purpose was thwarted by sin, but this does not alter the fact that this is why He made us in the first place, and why we are here.

The Bible not only teaches us to think of God as a Creator, but as a Father, and if wisdom and power are the marks of a Creator, then love is that of a Father. In fact, we are told that "God is love", and this indicates that man must have been created as an object of God's love, and that the chief reason for his existence is that he should respond to that love, and enjoy the unclouded friendship which ought to exist between Father and son.

4 | Can we trust the Bible ?

IT might be helpful to begin by stating what a Christian does *not* mean when he claims that the Bible is trustworthy. He does not mean that it has been dictated in some mechanical way by God, without regard to the personality of the individual writers, who have been reduced to the role of shorthand typists. He does not mean that its ideas about nature and the universe are compatible with twentieth century opinion, but rather that it was written against the background of contemporary belief and understanding. He does not mean that everything in the Bible is to be taken as literally true, but tries to discover what was the intention of any given writer. He does not believe that there is any one inspired and guaranteed interpretation of the Bible. He does not mean that as literature it sets a faultless standard of grammar or syntax; nor does he suppose that we possess a text today which is free of the sort of errors which are bound to arise as a result of frequent translating and copying. It is important to state this, because there are people whose picture of the Christian is a caricature, and who imagine him to believe all these things.

What the Christian does assert and believe is that the content of the Bible is absolutely to be trusted as expressing the mind and will of God; and that the form in which that truth is expressed, whether figurative or factual, does not in any way affect the complete reliability of the instruction given. He may, in fact, be unable to draw a precise line between the poetic, imaginative and symbolic on the one hand, and the factual on the other; but this does not matter, because the truths and principles conveyed, for example, in Genesis chapters 2 and 3, or the closing chapters of Revelation, are equally valid and authoritative even though it is impossible to say exactly where the symbolism begins and ends. In fact, the symbolism of the Bible is rather like the road signs we meet when motoring. Their pictorial presentation in no way alters our faith in the truth they are seeking to convey.

It is in this sense, therefore, that the Christian accepts the Bible as an authoritative guide in matters of faith and conduct, and turns to it with complete confidence, knowing that he will never be misled. That is not to say that his own interpretation of its teaching will be infallible. He will welcome the help which comes from centuries of understanding and experience, and the wisest contemporary reasoning he can find. It is rather like the Law which, although it is accepted as authoritative, requires very careful study and thought if we are to understand it properly, because its exact interpretation is sometimes in dispute.

Asked to support this belief in the Bible, the Christian does so in four ways. First, there is the faith which Jesus Himself had in the Old Testament, and which He urged upon His followers. He regarded what was written there as the utterances of God Himself, and His own constant reliance upon it and submission to it showed that He accepted its authority unreservedly.

Secondly, there are the claims which the Bible makes for itself. "All Scripture", we are told, "is given by inspiration of God"; and again, "Holy men of God spake as they were moved by the Holy Ghost". Moreover, this claim is supported by the internal evidence of the Book. Take, for example, the prophecies in the Old Testament which are fulfilled in the New; and the united voice with which it speaks on all the vital and fundamental matters concerning man's relationship with God.

In the third place it is important to add that many of the events in the Bible are supported by the findings of archaeology; and there are also scientists who find that as their knowledge of the universe increases, so too does their respect for the Bible, parts of which only begin to have meaning as we learn about the world God has created.

Fourthly, there is the power of the Book in the world. Think of its effect on individuals and on countries, bringing peace, strength and comfort down the ages. Think of its continued popularity, proved by the fact that more copies of it are sold and more translations made than of any other book. Think finally how it has persisted, despite attempts to stamp it out, and despite the fact that its readers have often been persecuted, imprisoned and slain.

5 | And what about the miracles?

IF we believe in a God Who created the universe, then clearly He is perfectly capable of interfering in the mechanics of His creation, and entitled to interrupt, when He wishes to do so, the natural order of things. On this assumption the problem is not perhaps why there are so many miracles recorded in the Bible, but why there are not more.

But there are certain related problems which need to be faced, and the first is this. If God is perfect, and at the same time in complete control of the universe, why is it ever necessary for Him to interfere in this 'supernatural way? First, it may well be that the coming of evil into the world threw everything out of joint, and that miracles are one way in which from time to time God redresses the balance. A driver in control of a car with faulty steering has to make certain adjustments which, if things were perfect, would be unnecessary. The second answer is that miracles are one way in which God is able to demonstrate His personal interest in the affairs of mankind, and by rescuing, guiding and protecting, to 'show Himself strong' on behalf of those who fear and love Him.

The next problem concerns the nature of the miracles themselves. It is argued that many of them, especially in the Old Testament, have a simple scientific explanation, while others, such as the healing miracles of Christ, can be explained on the grounds of psychotherapy. The fact that God used natural phenomena to perform great events need not surprise us. There may have been perfectly 'natural' explanations of some of the plagues of Egypt, or of the drying up of the Red Sea or the River Jordan; but that does not alter the fact that those present at the time attributed what happened directly to God in a way in which we perhaps have forgotten to do; nor does it alter the miraculous timing of these events.

Again, when we turn to Christ, it may be true that modern doctors and psychiatrists can produce cures similar to those which He worked supernaturally, but that does not make His own miracles of healing any less valid; nor does it affect the many others He performed in which He demonstrated His powers over nature, or those which concerned His own person—His birth, resurrection and ascension.

The third problem is this: Why do miracles no longer occur? Perhaps they still do happen more often than we realize. Many Christians have stories to tell of answered prayer, of solutions to problems and of the cure of diseases which, if less spectacular than those of old, are none the less real. Again, it is very hard for those of us who lived through the last war, for example, to believe that God had nothing to do with the escape of our armies from Dunkirk. The unaccountable way in which the German army was held back when it had our men at its mercy, the bad weather which temporarily grounded the Luftwaffe, the lake-like calm of the Channel—no wonder people still speak of 'The miracle of Dunkirk'!

But generally speaking it is probably true to say that the age of miracles is over, because their purpose has been fulfilled. We must remember that their chief purpose was always to reveal God's power, love and wisdom, and many were deliberate 'signs', or visual aids, by which God taught man about Himself. But with the return of our Lord to heaven, the revelation was complete. We have been given the full picture, and in the Bible we have all we need to know about the character and nature of God. So we find in the Acts, that although miracles were still performed by the apostles in the name of Christ, the direct and unmistakable occasions on which God intervened in the affairs of His people seem to become fewer.

The second purpose of the miracles was to increase man's faith—not so much to create faith where it did not exist already, but to nourish and stimulate what faith there was.

But here again, as the New Testament proceeds, we find a gradual change of emphasis, because, as their faith grew, the disciples became less dependent upon sight. "Blessed are they that have not seen, and yet have believed," said Jesus to Thomas; and Paul echoed those words when he said, "We walk by faith, not by sight". In other words, the need for miracles has to some extent passed, because the Bible itself now contains all the ingredients necessary for the development of a robust and lively faith.

6 | Is the Devil a real person ?

THERE can be no doubt at all that the Bible speaks of the Devil in very personal terms, giving him the name of 'Satan', which means 'adversary', and that Jesus Himself thought of him in the same way, and addressed him as a real person. No one, of course, believes the fairy-tale picture of him as some kind of monster with horns and hoofs; but it does seem likely, from hints that we get in the Bible, that he was once an angel who stood in God's presence, and that he rebelled against God and fell from grace. Ever since that time he has made it his business to try to oppose God's will and work, to promote evil and disaster, and to lead men and women into sin.

There is in fact so much evil in the world, that I myself have never found it difficult to believe in a personal devil. He leaves his footmarks and his finger-prints everywhere. But at the same time, we must be careful not to think of good and evil as two equal and opposite forces. This is what theologians call 'dualism', a kind of tug-of-war between God and the Devil, the outcome of which is still uncertain. From the very outset Satan has only been allowed to operate by permission, and for a limited period of time.

His eventual overthrow and destruction are certain.

There are in fact three ways in which the Bible spells out the defeat of Satan. *Fundamentally* he was defeated upon the Cross. The express purpose of Christ's coming into the world was "that He might destroy the works of the Devil". This destruction He achieved upon the Cross, when through the sacrifice of Himself, He cancelled for ever the consequences of sin. But though he is a defeated and mortally wounded foe, Satan has not left the field, and *practically* he can only be defeated when Christians, through faith and prayer, share in the victory which Christ has won for them upon the Cross. *Ultimately* his defeat will be celebrated when, in the vividly poetical words of the Book of Revelation, he is "cast into the lake of fire". On the Cross his authority was destroyed; through faith his power can be resisted; at the final judgment his presence will be removed.

The Bible tells us that there are two things about Satan which we need particularly to watch—his strength and his subtlety. There are times when he comes at us like 'a roaring lion', and there are others when he is 'transformed into an angel of light', and exercises all the cunning of a serpent. We need to be equally on our guard against the armoured thrust from in front, and the parachute landing in the rear.

To aggravate matters, the Bible indicates what we might call a 'Trinity of Evil'—the world, the flesh and the Devil. Continuing the military metaphor, we might say that while the Devil himself constitutes the main enemy, the world represents the allies which he finds on every hand, people who are offering no resistance to him; and the flesh (the sinful nature within us) is like the traitor within the gates, or the 'Fifth Columnist' as he was called during the war.

It is sometimes asked why, if God is perfect and almighty, He does not immediately put an end to the activities of Satan, and restore the world to its original state of harmony and peace. We must not doubt that He could do so, but for some good reason He allows things to continue as they are. It must in some way be for the greater glory of God and the ultimate good of mankind that Satan is allowed such

power, though it is made perfectly clear to us in the Bible
that his exercise of it is strictly limited and controlled.

But although the precise reasons are uncertain, and the
exact programme of events is difficult to trace, the great
fact remains that Satan's days are numbered, and that the
time will surely come when he will 'cease from troubling'.
It stands to reason, quite apart from what is revealed to us
in the Bible, that a world in which God reigns supreme,
and in which Christ is to be all in all, can have no place
for the Devil, and that he must be finally destroyed.

Both in the Old and New Testaments the Bible drops
hints about this blissful state of things. It tells us that even
nature, 'red in tooth and claw', will benefit from the removal of Satan's baleful influence; while in the closing
chapters of Revelation we are given a glimpse of the holy
city, from which all evil has been expelled, and where
"there shall be no more death, neither sorrow, nor crying,
neither shall there be any more pain".

7 | Was Jesus Christ the Son of God, or just a very good man ?

IT has always been the belief of the Christian Church that
Jesus was not just a very good man, but the Son of God;
that He did not begin His life when He was born into this
world, nor end it when He ascended into heaven; but that
He came from God, and returned again to His Father's
presence. This is a tremendous assertion, and if it could be
proved false, then the whole Christian religion would
collapse; for it stands or falls by what is called the 'Deity'
of Christ.

There is no doubt that Jesus claimed an equality with
God, and identified Himself with the Messiah spoken of in
the Old Testament. In a sense, therefore, the question we
are trying to answer does not arise; for if He was not the

Son of God, then He cannot have been a very good man, but either an impostor or a lunatic. But He certainly behaved like neither. Physically, He was a man of great courage and endurance. Intellectually, He could more than hold His own with some of the sharpest minds of His day. Emotionally, He was stable and balanced, sharing to the full the joys and sorrows of His fellow-men. Morally, as we shall see, He was beyond reproach.

This claim which He made for Himself was certainly believed by those who came to know Him best. Gradually they realized that here was no ordinary man, certainly no lunatic or impostor, but the 'Christ 'of Whom the Old Testament spoke, 'the Son of the living God'. And what was true then has been true ever since. Millions of people who have never seen Him have given Him their allegiance, and found Him to be, not just a wonderful example, but an active personal power, a living Companion and Friend.

Now this stupendous claim, made by Christ Himself, and on His behalf by His followers ever since, does not rest simply upon their own experience. It has a solid, objective and historical basis. First, consider His sinlessness. We never read of Jesus asking for forgiveness, because He never felt the need to do so. He claimed to be without sin, and neither His friends nor His enemies could point to the slightest trace of evil in His life. The question He once asked, "Which of you convinceth Me of sin?" went unanswered all through His life. Has it ever happened, before or since, that a man could live such a wonderful life that His two closest friends, writing about Him years afterwards, could say, "Who did no sin, neither was guile found in His mouth", and "in Him is no sin"?

Secondly, there was the authority with which He spoke. Everyone noticed this, long before they realized the full truth about Him. "Never man spake like this man," they said, as His words, like a sword, penetrated their heart and mind and conscience. He was not just another Moses, for He interpreted and amplified and even overruled the teaching of Moses. He was not just another Elijah, or one of the prophets, because He claimed to be speaking not only about God, or even from God, *but as God*.

Thirdly, let us consider the miraculous element in His life. There were miracles which He experienced (His birth, resurrection and ascension), and there were miracles which He performed. Are these not consistent with His claims? Are they not what we would expect to find if Jesus Christ was really what He claimed to be, God become man?

When trying to answer questions, one is on the defensive, but this time I want to come out of the corner, as it were, and force the 'unbeliever' on to the ropes. Can he prove to me convincingly that Jesus Christ was not what He claimed to be? He will find it a mighty hard thing to do. To start with, he will have to explain away the contemporary documents, dismissing them as forgeries, or as the product of deranged minds. He will then have to explain what fired and sustained the early Christians, and sent them joyfully to labour for Christ, accepting very often as their only reward persecution and death. He will have to find an alternative explanation for the experience of millions of present-day Christians, and for the growth of the Church during the last two thousand years. Finally, he will have to account in a satisfactory way for the fact that so much good has been done, and so many moral and social reforms have been inspired in the name of Someone Who, if He was not what He claimed to be, was either a crook, or at best a crank.

8 | Can we believe in the resurrection?

THE resurrection of Jesus is a very basic doctrine in the Christian Faith. If it could be disproved, then a number of other beliefs would be outflanked and threatened.

We would have to ask whether after all the death of Christ upon the Cross had been effective; whether there was any such thing as eternal life; and whether Christ Himself really was the Son of God. It is not surprising, therefore, that enemies of Christianity have made this belief one of their principal targets, and have been quick to point out what look like inconsistencies in the narrative, and the fact that nearly all the evidence is 'friendly', and comes from the followers of Jesus themselves.

It is when they try to advance alternative theories that they begin to run into trouble—theories, that is to say, which can account satisfactorily for the known facts of the case: the consternation of the Jewish authorities, the jubilation of the disciples, the remarkable spread of Christianity in its early days, in the teeth of opposition, and the subsequent growth of the world-wide Church. All these things require an explanation by those who dismiss the appearances of Christ to His followers as hallucinations brought on by wishful thinking and exaggerated rumour.

We can I think discount at the outset two of the more fanciful theories. The first of these maintains that Christ never actually died, but fainted, and then revived in the tomb and made His escape. In support of this it is argued that most men took hours and even days to die from crucifixion, whereas Jesus was buried the same evening. But quite apart from the fact that the centurion stated that He was dead, and Pilate specifically enquired whether He was, how could He possibly have recovered sufficiently to have escaped, even with help from outside, and then to have rallied His disheartened disciples? And if He did so, where did He go? How was the secret kept? There seem to be no grounds, either, for believing the second theory, that in the dim light of early morning the disciples went to the wrong tomb. Even if they did make this mistake, the authorities could easily have gone to the right tomb, produced the body, and put a stop to any idea of a resurrection.

We are therefore left with two other possible explanations. The first is that the authorities, Roman or Jewish, removed the body for reasons of their own—perhaps to prevent the disciples from doing so, or to forestall riots. It is difficult to believe that these were sufficient motives for their acting in this way, and there is no evidence to suggest that they did. In any case, we are still faced with the crucial question—why did they not produce the body when they saw that this disturbing belief in the resurrection was beginning to gain ground? One word from them would have quashed the whole idea. If for some inconceivable reason they kept silent, we have still to explain the astonishing growth and confidence of the Christian Church.

The other alternative is that the disciples themselves came and took the body away. This, you remember, was the story which the authorities themselves circulated, not because they believed it, but because in the emergency which faced them, they had to cook up some sort of explanation. But what possible motive could the disciples have had? And was it the kind of thing we can imagine their doing? Would they have had the courage? It seems very out of character, to say the least. And then, having done this, we are asked to believe that they perpetrated the most enormous hoax, which has lasted two thousand years, and for which men and women have gladly suffered every imaginable form of persecution. Is this reasonable, especially when we remember that it not only endangered the lives of the disciples themselves, but was a complete contradiction of their moral standards and teaching?

It seems as if the only possible explanation is the supernatural one which Jesus Himself foretold, and His followers have always believed. At some time in the early morning He rose from the dead, and passed out of the tomb. Then there appeared an angel (perhaps the 'young man' described by St. Mark) who rolled back the stone, not to release Christ, but to prove that He was already risen, by displaying the empty tomb and the undisturbed graveclothes. Apart from being precisely what the records tell us, this is the only theory which can account for all the facts as we know them to be.

9 | And what about the Virgin Birth? Where does that fit in?

IT is only within the last hundred years that people have started to challenge the doctrine of the Virgin Birth, the belief, that is, that Jesus had no human father, but that His conception within the womb of Mary was the work of the Holy Spirit. The attack has had two prongs, the historical and the theological. In the first place people have asked whether it actually happened, and in the second place they have asked if it matters whether it did or not.

It is perfectly true, as the critics point out, that apart from a few scattered hints, the only explicit references to the Virgin Birth are given us by Matthew (writing from Joseph's point of view) and Luke (writing from Mary's). But this silence on the part of the other New Testament writers is understandable. We can imagine that Joseph and Mary parted with the information very slowly and reluctantly, and then only to their closest friends; for, in the hands of the wrong people, it was the kind of secret which obviously lent itself to a scandalous interpretation. If Peter, John and Paul had nothing to say on the subject, it can only have been that the news had not reached them at the time, or that it was already being handled with a delicacy which made any further contribution unnecessary.

Moreover, it is clear that Joseph and Mary must have known their account to be true, or they would never have given it. If there had been the slightest possibility that Jesus owed His birth to Mary's intercourse with any other man, we can hardly imagine that they would have talked about it at all. We can be sure that they must have pondered these things long and anxiously, and it was only because they were completely satisfied in their own minds that the story they had to tell was the whole truth and nothing but the truth, that they released it to their friends.

It is, I know, arguable that 'parthenogenesis', as it is called, could happen as a freak of nature; but from what we know of the rest of the life of Jesus, it seems simpler to believe that His birth was due, not to some unnatural cause, but to a supernatural one, namely the direct intervention of God. This is certainly what Joseph and Mary believed, and is borne out by their experience of angels, prophecies and dreams.

But, some people may ask, does this doctrine matter very much? Would it not have been more in keeping with Christ's full humanity if He had been born in a perfectly natural way? I don't think we can argue that if He had been born naturally then He would not have been divine, but at the same time it must be admitted that at the very least the Virgin Birth was a remarkably fitting symbol or expression of His twofold nature. For if Christ was, as Christians believe, Son of God and Son of Man, human and divine, what could possibly be more appropriate than that He should have been "conceived by the Holy Ghost, born of the Virgin Mary"?

I think most Christians would go further, and assert that the Virgin Birth was not only a symbol, but was God's appointed way whereby Jesus inherited the two sides of His personality, the human and the divine. We must, of course, be careful not to think of Him as a kind of 'hybrid', for His two natures were not mixed, as are the nationalities of the child of a mixed marriage, but held together in perfect union and yet perfect independence. From first to last He was fully human and fully divine, God and Man.

There is also, as I see it, another reason why the birth of Jesus should have been "on this wise". It was God's way of proving that His Son had entered the world. If Jesus had been born in the normal way, then His parents might have been led to expect nothing unusual. As it was, they were warned and prepared from the start by this wonderful event, and they could plan accordingly. As Jesus grew in wisdom and stature, and when He became conscious of His ministry, how often Mary, and perhaps Joseph too, if he still lived, must have looked back to that miraculous start, and reinforced their own faith!

How long the secret remained theirs alone, we cannot say; but when gradually it came to be shared with others, we can imagine how it must have strengthened the faith of all who heard it. What could be more reasonable, they would ask, than that a life which had continued and ended on a miraculous note should have had a miraculous beginning? Is it not just what we would have expected?

10 | What is the Holy Spirit ?

WE must begin by rewording this question, for it should not be "*What* is the Holy Spirit?", but "*Who* is the Holy Spirit?" It is true that the New Testament itself sometimes refers to the Holy Spirit as 'It', but that is because the Greek word for spirit (pneuma) is neuter, and so the corresponding neuter pronoun was translated literally as 'it' and not as 'He'. But when we speak of the Holy Spirit, or the Spirit of God, we mean something very different from the 'spirit of Christmas' or the 'team spirit', that is, something generated amongst ourselves, an atmosphere of goodwill or fellowship. The Holy Spirit of God is the third Person of the Trinity. Someone Who is Himself God and is alive, available and active in the world today.

We may compare the Trinity to man himself, who is capable of thought, word and deed, and can think, speak and act, sometimes separately and sometimes all at once. God is like the Thought, at the back of everything there is; Jesus is the Word, Who gives expression to the Thought; and the Holy Spirit is the One Who translates it into Action and Who operates in the world today, invisibly, like the wind, but often with mighty effect. Or again, the

relation of the Holy Spirit to Christ is like that which exists
between a beam of light and the lamp from which it proceeds. The lamp in a lighthouse, for example, is stationary
and local, and its power is only experienced through the
beam which proceeds from it, and sweeps across the water.
So it is that the Holy Spirit spreads abroad the love and
power of Christ, and brings them home to the heart of the
individual Christian, wherever he may be.

When we turn from the nature of the Holy Spirit to His
work, we can, I think, say that He is active in two direc-
tions, in the world at large and in the Christian Church
in particular. In the first case He is an *Advocate*. That is
to say, He pleads God's cause in the mind and conscience
of men and women, reminding them of their need, and
pointing them to Christ as the Saviour. It is He, we are
told, Who came to "convict the world of sin, of righteousness and of judgment". It is He Who brings understanding
of the things of God. It is He Who is said to "strive with
man". It is He alone Who can perform the work of re-
generation in the human heart.

In the Christian Church, on the other hand, the Holy
Spirit is an *Ambassador*. Just as Her Majesty the Queen
is represented in Paris or Washington by an ambassador
who takes her place, and acts in her stead, so the place of
Christ in the heart of the individual believer and in the
Church as a whole is taken by the Holy Spirit. The Queen
cannot be everywhere at once, and the same, in a physical
sense, was true of Christ. His presence on earth was local
and temporary; the Spirit is universal and eternal. "Whither
shall I go from Thy Spirit?" asks the Psalmist, and after
visiting in his imagination the four corners of the earth, he
finds that "even there" he is in the presence of God.

But an ambassador is more than a representative, he is
also an interpreter. It is his task to convey and to explain
to the country to which he is accredited, the policy of his
own government. He does not create that policy, but he
expounds and interprets it. When Jesus was, so to speak,
introducing the Holy Spirit to His disciples, and outlining

the work He would do, He said this: "He will guide you into all truth . . . He shall receive of Mine, and shall shew it unto you." In other words, it is His job to make known and to interpret to the heart of the Christian the mind and the will of Christ.

Although since Pentecost we have been living in the 'Age of the Spirit', the period of history in which He is particularly at work, it would be a mistake to think of Him as only having come into the world at that time. There is plenty of evidence of His work in the Old Testament and in the Gospels. He was an agent at the Creation. It was He Who inspired the prophets, and empowered them to work wonders; and it was He Who was active at the time of Christ's birth, and throughout His ministry. Pentecost was not the beginning of His activity, any more than Christmas Day marked the beginning of the activity of the Son. It was simply the occasion on which He was poured forth in a unique way, and made universally available to mankind.

11 | What is the point of the Trinity ?

THE doctrine of the Trinity, although nowhere explicitly stated in the Bible, was finally adopted at the Council of Nicaea in A.D 325. The formula of 'Three Persons in one God' was an attempt to preserve two truths which become increasingly evident throughout Scripture. The first is that God is one. This truth, revealed to the Jews early in their history, distinguished their faith from every other contemporary religion, and has been inherited from them by Christians. The other, and apparently contradictory truth, was that God seemed to operate in three completely distinct ways, and that when He did, He did so as a Person.

The formula was drawn up not to resolve this contradiction, but to preserve it. It is tempting to try to find a solution to it. It would be quite easy in the first place to think of a God Who revealed Himself to mankind in three different ways. Just as you can have H_2O as ice or water or steam, so why can't you have God adopting three different roles—as Father chiefly in the Old Testament, as Son in the Gospels, and as Holy Ghost in the Acts? It is an attractive solution, but it won't do, and we have actually fallen into a heresy called 'Sabellianism'! It is true that we have preserved the unity of God, but we have thrown overboard the fact that He is three distinct persons, and not just one person in three different disguises.

The other attractive solution is to think of three separate persons in a kind of partnership or triumvirate. I can think of schools, for example, where there are three head-masters. One may be responsible for the discipline and curriculum, another for the estate and finance, and a third for the games and other out-of-school activities. But again, this will not do; for though there are three persons all right, each with his own sphere of activity, they are not one. They may work in great harmony, but we still have to speak about the 'Headmasters' in the plural. Unconsciously we have fallen into 'Polytheism'!

An illustration which may help occurred to me recently. Just north of Petersfield in Hampshire there is a short stretch of road which may fairly be described as 'triune', because within the unity of the road there are three separate and distinct routes—A3, A272 and A325—each of which has already functioned independently, and will do so again. But no illustration of this truth will bear much weight, simply because we cannot think of 'Persons' except as utterly independent beings, and the idea of having three such beings in one is quite outside our experience and understanding. The illustrations, like the formula itself, are perhaps most useful in showing us what to avoid, and in defining the frontiers we must not cross.

So far we have rather skated over the evidence in the Bible which led the Church to formulate this doctrine of the Trinity. It has been said that there is even a hint of it in the first three verses of Genesis. God the Father was the Thought behind the universe, God the Son was 'the mighty Word' at which creation 'sprang at once to sight', and God the Holy Spirit was the Principle animating the whole creation. When we turn from creation to redemption we find the same pattern. The conception of the plan was God's, its execution was the work of Christ, while its application to the individual is performed by the Holy Ghost. If we compare the Gospel to a great piece of music, it is as if the Holy Ghost is the Conductor, interpreting its glories to the human heart.

As the New Testament proceeds, it is perfectly clear that each member of the Trinity is thought of as being essentially God and a distinct Person. Jesus Christ, for example, is not spoken of as a very good man who was promoted at His baptism, but as someone who was eternally and completely divine. The Holy Ghost too is not thought of as an influence or an atmosphere, but as a Person, equal in status to the Father and the Son, but active in a different way from them.

These then are the grounds on which the early Christian Church was led to build this important doctrine. It is greatly to their credit that they did not try to evade it, nor did they seek an easy way out. They left us with one of the many paradoxes in the Christian religion which we must learn to accept by faith, even though we cannot grasp it intellectually.

12 | What will happen to me after death ?

THIS is not a subject on which we find every 'i' dotted and every 't' crossed in the Bible. There is a certain amount of reserve, and here and there some obscurity, due partly to the fact that it is not always possible to be sure whether we are to understand what we read symbolically or literally.

For example, it is not clear what will immediately follow death. St. Paul spoke of being 'with Christ', and the dying thief was given the same assurance, that he would be with the Lord that very day. Does that mean that we go straight to heaven, which is where other parts of the Bible tell us that Christ is reigning? Or into some sort of waiting-place, which is what Paradise is believed to be? Again, physical death is often spoken of as sleep. Are we therefore to be unconscious after death, and only wake up in time for the last judgment, when 'the trumpet shall sound'?

On these questions, and on the exact programme of events, Christian thinkers agree to differ, and perhaps speculation is unwise and unhelpful. But however that may be, there are certain other salient facts on which the Bible speaks with no uncertain voice, and which it emphasizes again and again. The first of these is the resurrection of the body. There are hints of this even in the Old Testament, but the full truth comes to light in the New, and finds its final proof in the resurrection of Christ.

Man is a spiritual being. That is to say, unlike the animals, he is equipped with a soul or spirit which, Christians firmly believe, has the capacity to survive death, when it will be clothed with another body, adapted to an entirely new kind of existence. Speculation as to the precise nature of this body will probably not get us far. It may be that it will bear no more resemblance to our present bodies than that of a butterfly does to the caterpillar from which it has developed. But the Bible clearly states that we shall be embodied spirits, able to identify each other, and certainly to continue an individual existence.

The second thing which is mentioned with complete certainty in the Bible is the final judgment. "It is given unto men once to die," we are told, "and after that the judgment." We can read about this in the Book of Revelation, where, in poetical language, the writer sees mankind standing before the throne of God. It speaks of the 'book of life' in which, it would appear, are written the names of all who have acknowledged Christ as their Saviour, and who are given a place in the heavenly city; while for those whose names are not in it there remains the bitter experience of expulsion from the presence of God because of their sins.

The third thing which emerges clearly from the Bible concerning life after death is that we shall see the final overthrow of Satan and all his works. In the late summer of 1940 the Germans used to say, "The war against England has been won; it is just a question of when it will be finished." How wrong they were, we now know; but the same remark applies very appropriately to the war against sin. The battle has been won on the Cross, and Satan is a defeated foe; but when will the war be finished?

It seems that the end will come in three stages. First, there will be universal acknowledgment on the part of mankind of the sovereignty of Christ when "at the name of Jesus every knee shall bow", and even those who have rebelled will be compelled to submit to His authority. Next will come the overthrow of Satan, and his final judgment and removal from the scene; and this will open the way for the end of all the evil things for which he has been responsible. There shall be "no more . . . sorrow, nor crying, neither shall there be any more pain"; "the last enemy that shall be destroyed is death", and Christ will be all and in all.

Of course, there remains a mystery about death, and just as we cannot see beyond the horizon, so exactly what lies beyond the grave is hidden from our eyes. But these three facts remind us that whatever else happens, Jesus Christ Himself awaits us there, our Friend, Judge and King.

13 | Do Christians believe that Christ will come again? If so, why has He not yet done so?

YES, Christians have always believed that Christ will come again "to judge the quick and the dead". The Bible leaves us in no doubt on this point, nor on the man-

ner of His coming; for it will be in marked contrast to His
first coming on Christmas Day. That was silent and secret,
and known only to a handful of people; but His second
coming will be visible and dramatic, as when a curtain is
suddenly flung aside to reveal someone beyond.

The purpose of His coming is also made perfectly clear,
and even if it were not foretold in the Bible, there is a
sense in which history and theology would require Him to
return, in order that His work might be completed. That
great event will in fact set in motion the whole programme
of the last days, leading up to the final judgment, the overthrow of Satan and all his works, and His own eternal,
triumphant reign. The Saviour will return as a Sovereign,
to conquer, to judge and then to reign for ever and ever.

The second part of this question is more difficult to
answer. If what has been said so far is true, and if the early
Christians lived (as they seem to have done) in almost daily
expectation of the Lord's arrival, how is it that we find
ourselves centuries later with the event still unfulfilled?

I think part of the difficulty arises from the fact that in
the gospels it is not always easy to tell whether Christ is
referring to His own return or to the forthcoming destruction of Jerusalem in A.D. 70. These two great events appear
to overlap and converge. It is rather like looking at two
mountains from a distance. From where you stand, they
look much closer together than they really are. This confusion of thought has sometimes led people to misunder-
stand our Lord's own teaching about His return.

Secondly, we would do well to study the answer of Peter
himself to this same question, "Where is the promise of
His coming?" He reminded his readers that from the divine
standpoint the arrival of Christ is always near, "for one
day is with the Lord as a thousand years, and a thousand
years as one day". God's time-scale is quite different from
ours. It is like the difference between an author and the
actor who takes the part of one of the characters whom he
has created. Five minutes' writing in the library may cover
several months or years upon the stage.

Next, I think there can be no doubt that it is part of God's purpose that each succeeding generation of Christians should live in the hope of the fairly immediate return of Christ. It is true that some may grow slack and cynical, and say, "My Lord delayeth His coming", and this may be part of His way of testing their sincerity; but for many more it acts as a spur and an incentive to higher standards and harder work. Christ Himself suggested this. Like a bridegroom returning from the wedding, He expects a *welcome* from His friends. Like a thief in the night, He expects a careful *watch* to be kept. Like a manager returning from a business trip abroad, He expects to find His employees faithfully at *work*.

Lastly, and from a general study of Scripture, it does seem that certain things have still got to take place before the return of Christ. Many feel that one necessary condition for His coming must be the preaching of the gospel throughout the world, an event which seems to lie still somewhere in the future. Others maintain that there must first be a great apostasy in the world, a deterioration of moral standards, a general falling away from God, and collapse of social and international relations. Some feel that an important prelude to Christ's arrival will be a spiritual revival of the Church, on a scale never seen before; while others believe that the Jewish nation will be included in this, and that on their part too there will be an unprecedented turning to Christ as their Messiah and Saviour.

Some of these 'signs' are hard to discern, and it would be unwise to be dogmatic. Again, some have appeared in the past, and not been followed by the arrival of Christ. What I think can safely be said is that the general trend of cosmic events seems to be in the direction indicated, and that our generation has perhaps more reason than any previous one to say, "The coming of the Lord draweth nigh". But having said that, do not let us fall into the trap of trying to establish a precise programme of events; for we are plainly told in Scripture that the exact time-table is not for us to know.

14 | Hasn't the Church failed? And why is it so disunited?

BEFORE we can make up our minds as to whether or not the Church has failed, we must ask ourselves what its true function is supposed to be. It was, of course, founded by Christ Himself, in order to carry on His work in the world after His return to heaven. It is in fact described in the New Testament as His 'Body', because now that He is no longer on earth. He carries on His work through the Church which is His agent in the world.

It is plain from the New Testament that the Church was entrusted with two main functions—worship and witness. In other words, its first job is to 'offer up' praise, thanksgiving and prayer to God; and its second job is to 'show forth' to the world at large something of the love and power and wisdom of almighty God. It is therefore in these respects that its success or failure must be judged.

Certainly no Christian will view the Church's achievement in either direction with pride or complacency. Its worship leaves much to be desired, and is often formal, empty and mechanical. Its impact upon the world, despite the fact that perhaps more than a tenth of the world's population is nominally Christian, and despite periods of spectacular progress, has been disappointing; and today, in the face of materialism, communism and other powerful national interests, it appears again to be losing ground.

On the other hand, I sometimes ask myself what the world would have become like if there had been no Christian Church at all. Many of the greatest social, moral, educational and medical advances have been inspired by the love of Christ, and pioneered, often at great personal cost, by Christian men and women; and there can be no doubt that, but for Christian people, the world would have developed much more slowly and expensively towards its present comparatively civilized condition.

Or again, if you could remove the Christian Church overnight, would it not make a stupendous difference for the worse? At one blow the traditions, restraints, standards and values which have been associated all down the years with Christianity would disappear; and though they have been taken for granted by some, and disregarded altogether by others, they have had a remarkably preservative influence upon society as a whole.

But if the world cannot afford the removal of the Church, it does require its revival. If only it could recapture permanently its original fire and power, as indeed it has done spasmodically through the centuries, then there is no telling how greatly God could use it to this sorely distracted world, bringing to it the sense of peace and purpose which it seems unable to find in any other direction.

One hopeful sign does lie, I think, in the many moves which are being made at the present time towards reunion of the various churches. Our Lord prayed so earnestly for this, and it must be a cause of great distress to Him, as well as shame to every Christian, that the Church is so divided.

I think it can fairly be said that the divisions are not always as deep or as permanent as they appear. Sometimes at the coast you see a number of rocks jutting out of the sea, each one apparently quite separate from and independent of the next. It is only when the tide goes out that you discover that they are in fact not separate rocks at all, but just different parts of the same reef. And the basic things which unite Christians are still far greater than those which divide them. In some cases the tide has withdrawn, leaving two churches which were divided, united in a new way. In other cases, it must be admitted that the seas of tradition, prejudice, misunderstanding and, let us face it, doctrinal error, have still a very long way to retreat. But at least we can rejoice in the fact that the tide has turned!

Meanwhile it is the duty of every Christian to work for a better understanding and a closer link with those from

whom he differs even on important matters, but with whom
he shares the same underlying and fundamental beliefs.

15 What is the difference between Roman Catholics and Protestants ?

FROM very early days the authority of the Bishop of
Rome was largely accepted throughout Christendom,
though in some places, notably in England, less rigidly and
enthusiastically than in others. After the great councils,
which decided many of the most knotty doctrinal problems,
such as the Trinity, power passed increasingly into the
hands of the Pope, and in the Middle Ages he became a
figure of great political and ecclesiastical importance. His
authority was immense, and at a time when the Bible could
only be read in Latin, the great truths it contained concerning Christian faith and conduct only reached the common
people after they were authorized by him.

Towards the end of the fifteenth century various streams
of thought—theological, cultural, moral and political—
arose and began to flow together. There was, for example,
an increasing dissatisfaction with the papacy. There was
criticism of some of its occupants, who lived notoriously
corrupt lives; while its practices also came under fire,
notably the sale of indulgences, whereby the penalties due
to sin could to some extent be relieved and remitted by the
payment of money. There was also that revival of learning
and culture known as the Renaissance, associated with which
were such people as Erasmus, and through which the Bible
came to be studied first in Greek and then in English.
There was finally a new spirit of nationalism which was
seen nowhere more strikingly than in the headstrong and
independent behaviour of Henry VIII.

All these influences found a focal point, a means of
expression and an intrepid champion in the person of a

German monk named Martin Luther. It was while he was on a visit to Rome that he had his 'Turmerlebnis' or 'Tower experience', when the light and truth of the Gospel dawned upon him for the first time. He became the 'father' of the Reformation, and from this point began the great break-away from Rome on the part of many of the northern countries of Europe, and the birth of the Protestant churches as we know them today.

The Council of Trent (1545–63) and the Counter Reformation did much to arrest this drift from Rome, and authorized a number of reforms within that church; but on all fundamental points it has remained as it was, and various doctrines pronounced since then have, if anything, only hardened the frontiers between Roman Catholics and Protestants.

In the eyes of Protestants, Roman Catholics are guilty of two principal theological errors. Others flow from them, but these two are fundamental. The first concerns the authority and, since 1870, the infallibility of the Pope. Those outside the Church of Rome have always protested that the Pope, by claiming to be the 'Vicar of Christ' on earth, is assuming powers and privileges which belong to Christ alone. They believe that Jesus never delegated His authority to man, but enshrined it for us in His Word, the Bible, from where the Holy Spirit conveys it to the believer.

The other cardinal error concerns the doctrine of 'Justification by Faith', that great truth which had lain hidden for so long, and which Luther rediscovered. The whole of Roman Catholic theology is really based upon the idea that we must use every effort—discipline, prayer, the sacraments—to make ourselves righteous and therefore acceptable to God. From this belief flows that stream of doctrine and practice which includes things like purgatory, the reverence paid to the Virgin Mary and the Saints, and above all the Mass, at which "the one perfect and sufficient sacrifice" of Christ is not simply remembered, but is repeated or re-presented week after week. Protestants, on the other hand, believe that they are reckoned righteous before

God by faith in Jesus Christ, quite apart from their own good deeds. These may express their gratitude to God for His forgiveness, but can never earn it.

There is no doubt that the gulf dividing the Protestant Churches from the Church of Rome is wider and deeper than that which separates any other group of churches, but even here there are signs of a new attempt at understanding. While it would be wrong to minimize these great and grievous differences, it is perhaps more helpful to end on a positive note, and to remind ourselves that even between Roman Catholics and Protestants there exist large areas of doctrinal and moral agreement.

16 | What is the point of the sacraments?

A SACRAMENT is an outward and visible sign with an inward and spiritual meaning – something we do which signifies what we think, or feel, or believe. A handshake, for example, is a sacrament of friendship, a kiss of love or affection, and a wedding-ring of marriage.

There are two sacraments which Christians use in this way to express spiritual truths connected with their faith, Baptism and the Lord's Supper, or Holy Communion. In Baptism we are figuratively cleansed from sin and rise again to newness of life; while in Holy Communion, by partaking of the bread and wine, we share symbolically in the death of Christ, and in the 'benefits of His passion'. Thus two of the most important things to do with our faith—our need of forgiveness and Christ's sacrifice for us—have been provided with outward and visible symbols.

It may be asked why we need sacraments at all. After all, we can be friendly with someone without shaking hands with him, so why can't we remember Christ's death without attending Holy Communion, and begin the Christian life

without Baptism? We can; but the fact remains that Christ
has commanded us to do these things, and that ought to be
sufficient reason. Perhaps He wants to use them as a form
of visual aid, because we all know that it is much easier to
understand and remember something which has been presented to us in a material and tangible way.

He also wants them to be what the Prayer Book calls 'an
effective sign'. This means that they are a sign or pledge
of an established relationship between God and ourselves,
and it means too that they not only express what is felt, but
in some way deepen the feeling itself. Thus a kiss will not
only express love, but increase it; and the sacraments are
ways in which our love for Christ and our trust in Him are
strengthened. We must remember too that these things are
not only a sign to ourselves, but to other people as well;
for just as the wearing of a tie or badge will denote a club
or regiment, so Baptism and Holy Communion are ways in
which we may show the world at large that we are wholehearted members of God's Kingdom.

There are certain dangers attached to sacraments. There
is the danger of formalism, when Baptism, for example, is
allowed to become little more than a social occasion and
the full significance of the act is overlooked and ignored.
Perhaps this is particularly the danger in countries where
it costs little or nothing to be a Christian, rather than in
those where Baptism requires a great deal of courage. In
England, for instance, it is easier to be baptized than to be
a Christian; but in many other parts of the world it is much
easier to be a Christian than to be baptized, and take an
irrevocable step which shows everyone the choice you have
made. The other danger is sacramentalism, when the visual
aid takes the place of the thing it is meant to signify, and
people tend to revere the symbol rather than the truth it
represents. In other words, wearing the tie and the badge
become more important and valuable than actually sharing
in the activities of the regiment. This attitude can lead to
a mechanical and even superstitious view of the sacraments.
But in between these two extremes they can serve a most

valuable and important purpose—reminding us of great things that have taken place; deepening our love, faith and courage and showing others what we believe and think.

It might be a help at this stage to say a word about Confirmation. This is the service by which those who belong to the Church of England are admitted to full membership, taking upon themselves the promises and vows which were made on their behalf at baptism. Other churches too have equivalent services by which the 'apprentice' becomes accepted as a responsible member of the Christian community, and is allowed to take a full part in its worship.

Here again, there is always the danger of misuse. Many young people are confirmed, for example, simply because they have reached what is felt to be 'the right age', regardless of their spiritual condition. But to mean anything at all, the outward ceremony of Confirmation, when we declare publicly our allegiance to Christ, must be matched by an inward attitude of love and faith towards Him. Seen in this light, and used in this way, Confirmation and other similar services are a splendid opportunity of showing other people Whose we are and Whom we serve, and underlining in our own hearts and minds our resolve to live for Christ.

17 | Is there literally a heaven and hell ?

I AM taking it that the word 'literal' in this context means actual or real, as distinct from metaphorical or figurative; and that the questioner is asking whether heaven and hell actually exist, or whether they are just a figure of speech, a kind of symbolism to describe two states of mind; or mythical, and on the same level as, say, Father Christmas.

There can be no doubt at all that in the Bible, and in the mind of Christ Himself, the terms 'heaven' and 'hell' represent real facts. Heaven is spoken of as the 'dwelling-place' of God, from which Jesus came to this earth, and to which He has now returned; and also the place which all who love Him will one day be allowed to enter. The usual word translated hell (Gehenna), on the other hand, is described as being the domain of Satan and his agents, and the place of retribution to which people go who refuse to repent of their sins and to turn to Christ.

It is true that a great deal of what is said about heaven and hell is couched in highly symbolic language and it is not always easy to see when we are dealing with a literal or a metaphorical description. But we must remember that the symbols stand for certain facts, and we cannot imagine that our Lord, for example, would have used metaphors which exaggerated the actual state of things as it is; and we must not be misled into supposing that a thing is less real because its meaning has to be conveyed to us figuratively.

This symbolism may or may not extend to the precise location of heaven ('up there') and hell ('down there'). Our present understanding of the universe makes these terms much less intelligible than they were to people who were brought up on a more elementary concept; but they certainly convey the right moral idea, and, after all, we still find it convenient to speak of 'sunrise' and 'sunset' although we do not pretend that these terms constitute a literal description of what happens every day. Again, we must not suppose that what is real must necessarily be material, and Paul warned us against this when he said, "the things which are not seen are eternal". The exact whereabouts of heaven and hell, and the actual form they take, matter much less than the fact that we are told that they exist.

The first thing that Scripture emphasizes about heaven and hell is that they are two quite distinct places. It is interesting to note that at the root of the Greek word for 'to judge' there lies this idea of separation—the sheep from the goats, the wheat from the tares; and heaven and hell represent the final phase of this judgment. The broad and the narrow way which were once two branches in the same road, have diverged so far that they have led men to irretrievable destruction or eternal life. In the second place the Bible stresses that there will be self-awareness in heaven and hell, and that we shall know where we are, why we are there, and what is happening to us; and in the third place it tells us that they are places of reward or retribution, as the case may be, and that we shall rejoice or mourn accordingly.

Understandably men have shrunk from the full implications of this doctrine, and attempted to soften it. Some prefer what is called 'Conditional Immortality', the idea that only those who turn to Christ qualify for life, and the rest become extinct, "dead in trespasses and sins". It is pointed out that Paul speaks more often of death than he does of hell, and that death suggests the absence of any form of self-consciousness. This view is plausible and attractive, but it must be admitted that the balance of Scripture is weighted heavily against it; and it could be argued that complete extinction of the individual contradicts the Christian view of the dignity and responsibility of man.

Others have turned to 'Universalism', the belief that ultimately all moral creatures, angels, men and devils, will share in the gift of salvation and be restored to God. The argument is that God can only be truly glorified and triumphant if such a restoration takes place. We are bound to say, however, that this idea, comforting though it may be, can find even less support in Scripture; and we must confidently believe that God's glory will be seen in the fact that He has acted, not in accordance with our wishes or hopes, but as a wholly righteous Judge.

18 | Don't science and religion contradict each other ?

A GREAT deal has been made of the so-called conflict between science and religion, though much less is heard about it today, partly because each has recognized the fact that it is called upon to operate in a different sphere; and there need be no conflict at all, unless one pronounces dogmatically in the sphere of the other. If, for example, because the Bible was written in pre-Copernican days, religion insists upon taking a pre-Copernican view of the universe, then science has a right to complain; and in the same way, for science to say 'this could not be', when faced with some miracle or experience it cannot explain, is equally impertinent. But in the ordinary way, if both observe the rules, there need be no more incompatibility between science and religion than there is between, say, geography and history.

Not only are they concerned with different spheres but, faced with the same phenomena, they tend to ask different questions. Science is concerned with 'how' things happen, and religion with 'why'; science with the cause, and religion with the purpose. For example, science may be able to give a very reasonable explanation for the cause of a rainbow or a sunset, but it cannot tell us why it is beautiful; that is a question which will only yield its secret to an aesthetic or perhaps philosophic approach.

"But surely," protests someone, "science can account for the origin of the universe in such a way that it makes the religious explanation unnecessary and indeed impossible. Hasn't science proved that everything came into existence spontaneously, and that there is no room behind the universe of today for belief in the sort of intelligent, personal God which religion seems to require?"

Not so at all. The present state of scientific knowledge compels an open verdict so far as the origin of the universe is concerned. The evidence of astronomers suggests that it is finite both in time and space, and if this is so, then it must have had a beginning. Because this beginning was a unique event, and incapable of being produced under the controlled conditions which would have made careful observation and measurement possible, it does not lend itself to the formation of any hypothesis which can be tested, and therefore verified or refuted. Speculations have been made by astronomers and others, but their truth or falseness cannot be demonstrated by the scientific method.

In other words, science on its own can tell us nothing about the origin of the universe, whether it was the result of spontaneous generation or special creation. If this question is to be answered at all, then the answer cannot fall within the sphere of scientific observation; nor can it be argued that what science has so far observed or recorded makes belief in the Christian idea of God impossible or unlikely. The most it can do is to say, "Not proven".

It is at this point that the Christian mounts the rostrum and asks to be heard. "If there is a God at all," he argues, "then you would expect Him to be a God Who declared Himself to His creation—a 'self-revealing God'. If He did not do so, then He would be a contradiction in terms, and we shall be quite happy to exchange Him for a mathematical formula. And this self-revelation is precisely what we claim to have happened at a given moment of history."

In other words, the Christian religion claims that a man called Jesus, Who lived nineteen hundred years ago in Palestine, behaved and acted as only God Himself could do, claimed that He was God, and was accepted as such by those who knew Him at the time and who heard of Him afterwards. Moreover, there are millions of people who have lived since then who claim to have experienced His help and comfort in their lives, to have enjoyed His answers to their prayers, and to have found in their faith in Him the mainspring of their existence.

The good scientist learns to keep an open mind about any subject under consideration, and only reaches his final conclusions after weighing and sifting all the evidence most carefully. Faced with these facts of religious experience, therefore, he will not, on insufficient evidence, jump to the conclusion that they are wrong, simply because he cannot explain them. On the contrary, he will tend to argue in this way to himself: "Unless I am in a position to disprove the existence of a God, I have no right to challenge the collective experience of those who claim to know Him."

19 | What can Christianity offer which Humanism can't?

HUMANISM is the belief that man has within himself the capacity for unlimited progress and self-betterment, and while he may derive great encouragement from the example and inspiration of good men, including Jesus Christ, he needs no superhuman power to help him to reach his ideals, and to produce a kind of heaven upon earth. In this philosophy sin is not regarded as an ingrained bias towards evil, but simply as the unfortunate product of hereditary environment, or perhaps glandular disturbance. Put these things right, and man will gradually 'move upward, working out the beast', until the perfect being is evolved.

It was towards the end of the last century that Humanism began to gain such widespread popularity, even affecting a good deal of Christian thinking. It received a very severe setback during the two world wars, especially the second, when the horrors of Belsen and Auschwitz gave colour to the remark attributed to the First Duke of Wellington, "Educate men without religion, and you will merely make them into clever devils". But Humanism has always refused to accept this realistic view of human nature. Individual waves may retreat, but it believes that the tide is still coming in; and encouraged by the creation of the Welfare State and scientific advances, its popularity in recent years has enjoyed considerable revival.

Now if Humanism is right, then the claim of the Christian Gospel to be the only hope of man's salvation, and the unique solution to his problems, is hopelessly undermined. We must therefore examine its credentials very critically and closely.

First, it claims to be working for the ultimate good of mankind, and towards a point where there will be no more

47

sin. It would be churlish to belittle the enormous amount
that humanists have done to improve the lot of mankind,
but have they in fact made better men and women? Have
the war on poverty, the advance of medical science and the
creation of organizations like UNESCO resulted in any
marked improvement in the character of man? There is no
evidence to suggest that they have. True, modern man is
less uncouth than his ancestors, and sins in a more refined
and sophisticated way, but is he really kinder, less selfish,
purer, humbler? And if he is, is that improvement not
attributable chiefly to the influence of Christianity?

Again, Humanism has no message for the present generation. The improvement it expects is so gradual and slow
that many generations must pass before there can be any
perceptible result to show for its efforts. If it claims, as it
does, to have a message for every man, isn't this a miserable
commentary—that generations must be sacrificed and
millions must die before its Utopia is achieved?

And what about the greatest and most inescapable of
human problems—death? Has Humanism anything to say
about that? No! All its efforts are directed towards material
welfare and to giving man a better time on earth, although
in doing so it removes one of the chief incentives to the
very improvement it seeks, namely the prospect of having
to give an account of ourselves and our lives to God.

It is at these very three points that Christianity has something positive and definite to offer. "Man", it says, "is basically evil, and left to himself will drift downwards. Improv-
ing his environment won't help. If you keep a pig in the
drawing-room, which is the more likely result—a well-
mannered pig or a 'shambolic' drawing-room?" That is its
assessment of human nature; but it goes on to show that
Christ can give a new nature and a new power, and produce the sort of life which everyone, including humanists,
considers so desirable.

Christianity also has a message for this generation. For
those who will hear and receive the Gospel there are the
very things here and now which Humanism offers in the

distant future. Christ offers His followers peace, power and
joy which makes them less dependent upon material advantages, and yet at the same time generates that spirit of
industry and thrift which makes the acquisition of those
advantages more rather than less likely.

Finally, Christianity speaks with a positive and reassur-
ing voice about the future; for it claims that physical death
is not the end, but that there is a life for which this present
one on earth is but a prelude and a preparation.

20 | Aren't all religions equally true? Why should Christians suppose that they are right, and that everyone else is wrong?

THERE can be no doubt at all that Christianity claims to
be not merely one among many religions, nor even the
best on the market, but the only true religion there is.
Jesus said, for example, "I am the way, the truth and the
life; no man cometh unto the Father, *but by Me*". Either
what He said was true, or it was false. If it was true, then
other religions, however high their ethical standards and
however noble their teaching, cannot provide a way for
man to reach God. If it is false, then obviously the very
foundation of the Christian Faith is destroyed, and the
whole thing stands hopelessly discredited. In other words,
this uniqueness is not what Christians claim for their religion, but what its Founder Himself claimed. Everything
therefore in the last resort must turn upon the validity of
His claims, which are studied elsewhere in this book.

Meanwhile let us examine the effects of the great religions of the world upon mankind, and see whether on
purely practical grounds Christianity can fairly be regarded
as unique. We may I think begin by noting that its appeal
has always been universal. Most of the great religions
of the world have been or are associated with certain

geographical areas—Buddhism and Hinduism in Asia, for example, and Mohammedanism throughout the Middle East. While it is true to say that Christianity has progressed most noticeably in the western hemisphere, yet wherever it has been free to do so it has proved its power to transform individuals and influence nations.

The reason for this is that Christianity alone can provide the solution to some of the deepest and most pressing human needs. It claims to be the one and only answer, for instance, to the moral problem of human sin. In Jesus Christ it offers mankind a Saviour from the past effects of sin, and Someone Who can give the power to conquer it in the future. No other religion has any answer to this most intractable of all problems.

Next, we are bound to ask ourselves how the different religions of the world compare with each other in their approach to the problem of suffering and pain. Christianity sees suffering as a consequence of sin, and the result of Satan's interference in the world. Therefore, following the example of their Master when He was on earth, Christians try to relieve it wherever it appears. This is not so with other religions. The Muslim sees it as 'Kismet', the will of God, and not to be interfered with. Perhaps this is why medical missionary work has made such limited progress in many Muslim countries. The Hindu also, with his fatalistic doctrine of Karma, adopts much the same attitude.

Again, what about man's social problems? Take the relationship between men and women. In the eyes of the Muslim, for example, a woman is the mere chattel of the man, and in the Koran she is permanently branded as inferior. But how differently Jesus treated women! In the sight of God men and women are equal, and there is neither 'male nor female'.

Take what we might call the personal problem of individual destiny. Both Hindu and Buddhist claim that man's independent, separate personality is lost for ever when he dies, in the nothingness of Nirvana. Christianity on the other hand is the religion of the individual, and much of

Christ's time and many of His stories were concerned with the one person who was in need of help; while the Christian also believes that the individual personality will survive the physical disintegration of death.

Of course, it is true to say that all religions, including Christianity, have much in common, and are all attempts to establish a relationship between man and God. This means that the missionary method and approach tends nowadays to begin by discussing the common ground between all religions, whether doctrinal or ethical, before examining the divergencies. But when the fork in the road is reached, Christians believe that theirs is a religion revealed by God, while all the rest are natural. The quest of all religions is, "Canst thou by searching find out God?" The answer of the Christian is, "No, not by searching", *but by Christ alone.* This is not a position he would seek to hold with intellectual arrogance, but it explains why basically he must feel that his own belief is opposed to and incompatible with that of every other religion.

21 | Do Christians believe in re-incarnation?

THE belief that man may have more than one existence on earth, and not necessarily always in human form, is still very widespread in India and the Far East, where it forms part of the Buddhist and Hindu faith. The idea is that souls migrate from one body to another until complete purification is achieved, when they are finally released altogether from their earthly state.

In pre-Christian days the most notable exponents of this theory were perhaps Plato and Pythagoras, while it was also believed by many of the later Jews. After the coming of Christ, it was attacked by leading Christian thinkers, chiefly St. Augustine, and was condemned at various councils.

More recently it has enjoyed some revival through the spread of such cults as theosophy and spiritualism.

The particular attraction of this belief lies in the fact that it offers some sort of satisfying explanation for the desperate inequalities which we see amongst mankind. If it can be believed that someone starting life under a terrible physical, mental or social handicap in some way owes his misfortune to his pride, greed or cruelty in a previous incarnation, then it is felt to be less arbitrary and unfair.

It is interesting to note that the disciples of Jesus, infected by, or perhaps merely echoing, the current Jewish teaching, once asked Him a question on this point. Faced with the inexplicable tragedy of a man born blind, they asked, "Who did sin, this man or his parents, that he was born blind?" While not explicitly denying the transmigration of souls, Jesus' answer emphatically exploded the principal reason for believing it, by showing that there was no such connection as the disciples had implied between suffering and sin.

Not only in the teaching of Jesus, but throughout the Bible we look in vain for any hint or suggestion of this theory. One or two passages have been quoted in support, like the one in Psalm 51 where the writer says, "Behold, I was shapen in iniquity; and in sin did my mother conceive me". But Christians have always taken this to mean that everyone born into this world inherits a nature which is infected by sin. The Bible certainly warns us, too, that our sins can be 'visited upon our children'. But that should be obvious. A cruel, drunken, extravagant father will clearly harm and damage his children, perhaps permanently, and this may be part of his earthly punishment for such behaviour; but that is very different from the doctrine that the conditions of our present existence are determined by our behaviour in an earlier one.

Nor is there any scientific evidence for this belief. Sometimes it is argued that dreams supply one, and that in them we visit places we do not know, and which must therefore form part of the background of a previous incarnation. But it is far more likely that they spring from the subconscious mind, where things lie hidden which we shall never remember, or from a lively imagination; or is it conceivable (and I once had a question on this point answered by a BBC 'Brains Trust') that we can inherit ideas?

The two great things for which the doctrine of re-incarnation pleads are given a perfectly satisfying and positive answer in the New Testament. There is first of all the question of personal survival. In many places this is emphasized in the Bible, but such survival is always connected with some sort of spiritual existence, in heaven or in hell; and it is always associated with a body which has been specially prepared for that purpose, and never in any sense with one which is physically earth-bound.

The other belief, namely that of rewards and punishments, is intimately woven into the Christian teaching on judgment. The Christian believes that we shall all be accountable to a completely righteous Judge Who will understand our circumstances and the disadvantages under which we have lived. This is surely preferable to a system of justice which would punish the wicked by making it easier for them to be worse, and reward the good by making it easier for them to be better.

We are left, it is true, with the problem of unmerited human suffering on our hands, but here again, we are safer off with no logical explanation, but faith in a God of love, than we are with one which is incompatible with Scripture, and which brings a host of further problems in its wake.

22 | Does it matter what I believe so long as I am sincere?

IT has been suggested that the word 'sincerity' comes from two Latin words meaning 'without wax'. This is doubtful, but the idea is a good one; for a sincere person is one whose life has no thin veneer of wax, but is the same all through—genuine, frank and honest. He is not hypocritical, nor does he act a part; but his deeds match his words, and his behaviour his beliefs. Therefore, in itself, sincerity is a very desirable Christian virtue.

But the question we are considering suggests that the most important thing in life is not what we believe, but the sincerity and intensity with which we believe it; and the questioner probably has in mind the fact that there are so many religions in the world, and they all have some good in them, that it does not matter very much which one we choose, or whether we choose any at all, so long as we live up to what we believe. Now of course it is probably better to live like an atheist, if you are one, rather than to pretend to be a Christian, and in this sense a sincere atheist is preferable to an insincere one; but to say that it does not matter what we believe so long as we live up to those beliefs is rubbish, as we can see at once if we apply this idea to things like medical science and mathematics. I may believe with the utmost sincerity, for example, that arsenic is the perfect cure for hay-fever, or that five times six make fifty; but if I act upon those beliefs, I am going to land myself in all sorts of trouble.

It is perfectly true that there are some things about which it is perhaps not necessary or important to have exact beliefs, either because they can have no possible effect upon my daily life, or because the data are at present inadequate. For instance, it probably does not make very much practical difference to my life what I believe about space, whether it is limited or not, and in any case I do not know enough about it to be able to decide. But it is a very different matter indeed if the things we are considering provide us with the necessary data, and are intimately concerned with our day-to-day living and our final destiny. Our beliefs can then be a matter of life and death.

In cases of this sort we can, I think, go so far as to say that a man who sincerely believes what is wrong is in a far more dangerous condition than the man who holds the same beliefs, but hesitatingly and with many a doubt. If I am motoring confidently along the wrong road, I am much worse off than the man who is following me, but who is always stopping to ask the way. I know we are told that 'ignorance is bliss', but that is a dangerous half-truth. It may apply in cases where the truth can never or will never be known; but if one day it leads to disillusion, then it is anything but bliss. We have only to read the early life of Paul to see how much more dangerous a man can be if he is sincerely mistaken rather than just mistaken.

Applying all this to the realm of religious faith, it must be said that what is of chief importance is not the sincerity of my beliefs, but their object; not how I believe, but what I believe. Even faith as a grain of mustard seed in the right object is better than the most passionate belief in the wrong object. I am far better off groping my way blindfold along the right road, than bowling blissfully and confidently along the wrong one.

Now this attitude of false optimism is not really sincerity at all, but is only masquerading as such. The sincere person will ask himself two questions. First, what are the data of the Christian Faith, and are there sufficient grounds for believing it? Secondly, if Christianity is true, then does it matter whether I believe it or not? In other words, his sincerity is going to show itself in a very careful examination of these two things—the reality and the relevance of Christianity. Does it belong to the group which we have illustrated from medical science, from mathematics and from travelling? Or does it belong to the other group concerning the precise nature of the universe and the performance of celestial bodies? In other words, my sincerity will show itself first of all in the single-mindedness and intensity with which I seek and try to discover the truth; then in the conviction with which I hold it; and then in the whole-heartedness with which I practise it.

23 | Do we have a second chance? And what about the heathen?

THERE is no suggestion in the Bible, nor any logical reason for supposing, that those who have consciously and deliberately rejected the claims of Christ in this life will be given a further chance to accept them in the next; nor that they would take advantage of it if they were. The explicit teaching of Scripture on the subject is that it will be on the deeds and decisions of this life that we shall be judged, and that there is 'a great gulf fixed' between the kingdom of darkness and the kingdom of light which can only be crossed on this side of the grave.

But having said that, I think it is only fair to put the supplementary question, 'What constitutes a *first* chance?' Are those to whom the gospel has never been preached, or who have never had the opportunity of understanding it, to be judged on the same basis as those who have heard it, understood it and categorically rejected it? What about those who die in infancy, or those who are mentally defective, or the heathen? Will they not be given a further opportunity?

There are hints in the Bible that no one will be condemned for ignorance of what it was impossible for him to know, and that the Law or conscience will be the standard by which many are judged; but the reply to these questions must be that we know too little to say: too little about the mystery of hereditary sinfulness, and of the degree of responsibility involved in the completely unenlightened conscience. We must remember that the judgment is not in our hands, but God's, that He is both legislature and executive, and that 'the Judge of all the earth' will infallibly 'do right'.

In this connection I have often been asked what the position is of those who lived in the Old Testament days, before the coming of Christ. It is clear that those who were taught to worship the one, true, living God were accepted on the grounds of their faith in Him; a faith which was counted to them for righteousness, because it was of the same quality as that which in New Testament days led people to put their trust in Christ as their Saviour.

The reticence of the Bible on this whole subject is tantalizing, and we could wish to know more, and with greater certainty. But it is clear that if we had grounds for believing that the heathen, whether living in China or Britain, were in no sort of spiritual danger, then one of the greatest incentives to all evangelistic and missionary work would be removed. Without committing itself in any way as to the final destiny of such people, the Bible makes it perfectly plain that those who have heard the gospel, and taken the opportunity of accepting it, are immeasurably better off, even in this life, than those to whom it has never been preached. The Christian regards himself as a doctor with some life-saving drug in his pocket which he dare not withhold from someone in need on the off-chance that he may recover by some other means at a later date.

Paul emphasizes this over and over again. It is interesting that he refers to himself as a 'debtor'. He felt he owed men something—not money (he was always very careful about that), but the Gospel. It is easy sometimes to slip into that attitude of mind in which the Christian regards himself not as a debtor, but as a benefactor, bestowing upon people the delightful luxury of the Gospel, a valuable optional extra, but not a basic necessity. Nothing could be further from the point of view of the Bible. Those without Christ are never depicted as being simply unfortunate, but as being in desperate need; not as pupils, who need a little encouragement and coaching, but as patients, who are in danger of perishing. They are said to be 'without hope', 'alienated from the life of God', and lying 'in the power of the evil one'.

In His infinite mercy, justice and wisdom, God will doubtless have the perfect answer to all the questions we have raised, and we must be content to leave it with Him; but whatever those answers prove to be, they can never relieve us of the debt we owe to our fellow-men and women. Putting it even at its lowest, it is better by far that they should live this earthly life in the light of the glorious assurance of sins forgiven, than in the dim twilight of uncertainty and doubt.

24 | If God is both almighty and loving, why is there so much suffering in the world ?

IT is well to begin by distinguishing between two kinds of suffering. There is the sort which can be traced, either directly or indirectly, to man's sinfulness and rebellion against God. War is a good example of this. It arises directly from greed, lust and hatred; and if man had never sinned, and was incapable of these things, then there would be no war. The problem which faces us here, therefore, is not so much the problem of suffering as such, but the problem of evil. Why should a loving and almighty God allow sin to enter the world in the first place?

God could have made us like robots, incapable of doing anything that was wrong. Why then did He not do so? Why did He take the apparently fearful risk of giving us free wills? If God is love, then He requires the response of love from man, and this in turn involves the gift of free will, and the possibility of its misuse. Furthermore, if God is almighty, then in some way man's failure must lead ultimately to the good of His creation and to His own glory, even if we cannot see precisely how. It is arguable, for example, that before the Fall man was merely innocent, but that as a result of the Fall, and by overcoming temptation, he has had the chance to become righteous, which is something very much better. It is certainly true that but for the Fall, Christ would not have come into the world as Re-

deemer, and therefore the fullness of God's love would
never have been known. "O happy sin which has deserved
to have so great and so mighty a Redeemer."

But while these thoughts may help towards an understanding of the problem of evil, they do not appear to
touch the second kind of suffering which faces us, namely
that which cannot in any sense be attributed to man's sin—
the thalidomide baby, the patient suffering from an in-
operable cancer, the family shattered by some appalling car
accident. What are we to say about these? Perhaps they are
not as remote from the problem of evil as we think, because
we live in a fallen world, and there is a sense in which the
whole creation has been twisted and dislocated by man's
sin. But having said that, what positive help can we give to
people caught up and involved in this kind of experience?
It is tempting to shrug one's shoulders and say, "It is
beyond me. I can't cope". But that is a cowardly way out.

We can talk, in the first place, about the unsearchable
wisdom of God, the fact that He knows best, and that somehow, somewhere we shall come to see that "behind a frown-
ing providence He hides a smiling face". Does that sound
trite and shallow? Not to those whose faith in God is
strong. They do believe that "all things work together for
good to them that love God". Their faith has not simply
survived the fire, but like gold, it has come out all the
stronger and purer; and they know that in God's good time,
if not in this life then in the next, they will come to see
His pattern and His plan.

Secondly, pain and suffering very often serve as 'God's
megaphone', His way of calling us back to Himself. When
everything is going smoothly and well, it is all too easy for
us to trust in and even idolize material things. Sometimes,
in order to call men back to Himself, God has to strip us of
these things one by one. This was the message of the Book
of Job, though Job was an example of a man who had not
made this mistake, and God used him as a demonstration
rather than as a warning. There must be countless Christians in the world today who never heard or heeded God's

whispered warning to their conscience, but who have begun to retrace their steps to Him because He called to them loudly and clearly through suffering or pain. In fact, He has shown His love to them by allowing these things, and by using them to restrain, to recall and to teach.

Thirdly, there can be no doubt that those who have suffered and have learnt to accept their suffering as part of God's will for their lives, have gained something which others do not seem to acquire, and which perhaps can be found in no other way. It is not only that their faith has been strengthened, and their walk with God has become closer, but also that they have inherited from their suffering a poise, a calm, a sympathy and understanding which make them the sort of people to whom others turn instinctively when in trouble and distress.

25 | If God knows everything that is going to happen, how does it make any difference what I choose?

In many places the Bible makes it perfectly plain that God has complete foreknowledge. Indeed, this should be obvious; for it is unthinkable to imagine a God Who is almighty in every respect, and yet Who can be taken by surprise, because He does not know what is going to happen in the future; though we must remember that in one sense He stands outside time altogether, and that with Him there is no past or future, but only an eternal 'Now'.

This relation between foreknowledge and freedom of choice has never in itself greatly worried me. I cannot see why the fact that my future actions are known need in any way affect my freedom in making them. After all, foreknowledge is really only memory working the other way. My memory of what I did this time last year does not alter the fact that I acted quite freely; so why should God's knowledge of the future affect my freedom of action then?

But I realize that this is only one aspect, and perhaps the simplest, of a much more complex problem; for the Bible speaks not only of God's foreknowledge, but also of His predestination, or determinism. In other words, what happens is not only foreknown, but fore-ordained. It would be all right if His determining of the future sprang from and depended upon His foreknowledge of it, but unfortunately the best Christian thinkers will not allow that; and, whether we like it or not, we are faced with a rather disturbing paradox, that God has ordained everything that will happen, but without robbing us of a vestige of our free will.

The Bible is equally emphatic about both truths. There are passages where it is made perfectly clear that in His sovereignty God must determine the course of the world, and of individual men and women from start to finish; and there are other passages which emphasize with equal force man's complete personal responsibility. Is the Bible contradicting itself? I do not think so for a moment. What it is doing is to give equal and proper weight to two truths which from a human point of view cannot be reconciled— the sovereignty of God and the responsibility of man; but the fact that they are humanly irreconcilable does not mean that they are irreconcilable to God. They are like the two pillars of an archway meeting in heaven, above the fogs of human wisdom and understanding; or like the proverbial parallel lines which only meet in infinity. We think we are holding two ropes, one in each hand, whereas we are in fact holding two ends of the same rope which passes beyond our limited knowledge right into the unfathomable wisdom of God. Faced with this sort of problem, we must avoid two mistakes.

The first mistake is to try to tie the two ends together by finding some facile middle course which appears to reconcile both truths. Scripture itself eschews this easy way out, giving us both extremes with an uncompromising starkness and clarity. That is why analogies are apt to be dangerous; they tend to suggest a human answer to a problem to which there can in fact only be a divine answer.

The other mistake which many people have made, and which has led to controversy and division, is to imagine that the truth lies at one extreme or the other. Even two such great men as Wesley and Whitfield fell out over this, Wesley stressing the absolute freedom of man's will, and Whitfield the sovereignty of God.

We must always remember that in problems of this sort the truth lies, not at one extreme or the other, and certainly not in some sort of synthesis between the two; but it lies at both extremes at once. We might compare it to the use we make of electricity. If you connect only one wire, you will produce no light or power. If you join both wires together, you will blow a fuse, and plunge yourself into darkness and confusion. But if you use both wires separately and simultaneously, even if you do not understand exactly how it works, all will be well. In the same way we must learn to believe with equal tenacity in the sovereignty of God and the responsibility of man. We may not be able to explain the why and the wherefore, but we shall be conforming to the practice of Scripture, and we shall generate spiritual light and warmth.

26 | How would you define a Christian ?

THERE are two popular answers to this question which we must consider for a moment. Many people define a Christian as someone who is born in a Christian country, and has the advantages of a Christian upbringing and education. There is no doubt about the value of these things, but they do not of themselves make a person into a Christian, any more than it follows that I am white because I am born in Europe, or look like a horse because I happen to have been born at Newmarket.

Others maintain that a Christian is one who performs

certain religious duties—says his prayers, reads his Bible, goes to church, and so on. A good Christian does do these things, but he does them because he is a Christian, and not in order to make himself one; just as a man does not wear a special uniform in order to make himself into a policeman, but because he is a policeman already.

Just as there are certain 'hall-marks' which distinguish silver from other metals, so there are certain basic things which distinguish the Christian from every other kind of person. The first of these is that *he believes in Christ*. There are many who do this in the sense that they believe that He lived and died, and that He was perhaps the greatest Person Who has ever been, but the Christian goes very much farther than that. He believes that Jesus Christ is the Son of God, or God manifest in human form. This conviction, although he is confident that it can be supported by the strongest possible reasons, is not one which he has necessarily arrived at in the first place intellectually. It has been brought home to him, revealed to him, he would say, by the Holy Spirit. He has come to see, as Peter did, that Jesus of Nazareth is more than a Carpenter, more even than a Prophet; that He is in fact "the Christ, the Son of the living God", an eternal, immortal Person, with all the stupendous implications that follow.

Secondly, he is someone who *belongs to Christ*. This follows naturally from what we have just seen. If Christ is the Son of God, then He claims our love and our allegiance; and our natural, inevitable response must be to submit to His claims, turning to Him as a Saviour from sin, as a Guide in our daily life, and as Lord and Master of our souls. We all know what it is to 'belong' to something—a family, a team, a club or a school. It means that for various reasons those things have first claim upon our loyalty and affection. That is what it means to belong to Christ.

But by what right does Christ lay claim to our lives? He does so on two grounds—creation and redemption. Imagine an artist who, with infinite care, paints a picture of which he is justly proud, only to return home to find it has been stolen. A long, sad search begins, and then one day to his astonishment he finds it in a shop full of antiques, damaged, disfigured and marked 'for sale', but unmistakably his. Explanations follow, but in the end a price is demanded and paid. Once again the painting passes into the hands of its rightful owner, and is carefully and lovingly restored. Who can doubt with what pleasure and affection the artist would show it to his friends, for now it belongs to him twice over. It is his by creation, and it is his by redemption. And these are the two reasons why Jesus Christ asks for the wholehearted allegiance of our hearts and lives, and wants us to belong exclusively to Himself.

The third mark of the Christian is that *he behaves like Christ*. In other words, Christianity affects a man in three ways—his head, his heart, and now his hands. This stands to reason. If I believe in my doctor, then I am very careful to obey his instructions. If I belong to a certain team, then I am determined to fight its battles, wear its colours, and uphold its standards. And if I believe in Christ and belong to Him too, then I shall do all in my power to live the kind of life which is pleasing to Him and consistent with my profession as a Christian; a life in which there is increasingly less room for what is sinful and unworthy, and in which all that is pure and honest and true is assiduously cultivated.

Such a life not only gives practical expression to my faith in God, but also commends it to others. I wonder whether you are ever influenced by advertisements which you see, for example, on TV. Do you sometimes see an article presented so attractively and convincingly that you say, 'I must get that at once'? I confess it does not very often happen to me like that; but that ought to be the effect of our Christian witness upon others.

27 | Why is the Bible always harping on sin ? What is it anyway ?

WHAT would you expect? Sin is perhaps the most universal fact of experience there is. Many people manage to go through life without meeting serious illness, accident or misfortune, but everyone sins; and no book, therefore, which claims to deal with the nature of man and his relationship to God can possibly avoid the subject. You might as well expect a book on medical science not to mention disease. But it is important to add that the reason why the Bible has so much to say on the subject is a positive as well as a negative one. Not only does it condemn sin in clear and unmistakable terms, but it offers a cure for it as well; for its chief purpose is to tell of God's remedy for sin and His redemption of mankind.

I hope that is all that need be said by way of an answer to the first part of the question, and that we can now turn to the second, which asks what sin is. The Bible usually makes a distinction between 'sin' and 'sins'. 'Sin' is an infection which has found its way into human nature and poisoned man's whole moral system. As a result of this, he commits individual 'sins', perhaps murder, theft, adultery and the like. 'Sin' is the root and 'sins' are the fruit. In other words, we are not sinful because we commit sins, but we commit sins because we are sinful by nature.

And so the problem has to be dealt with on two levels. Let us consider 'sins' first. They are of three kinds. First, there is moral failure, or *'coming short'* of God's standard. In the words of the Prayer Book, "we have left undone those things which we ought to have done". This is actually the original meaning of the word 'sinner'. It meant someone who had missed the target; and Paul describes sin in one place as falling short of the glory of God, and failing to reach His standards of purity, love, honesty and humility.

The second kind of sins may be described as *'turning aside'*. Very often the word 'iniquity' (= 'unequal') is used for this particular kind of failure, and it refers to man's innate selfishness, and desire to go his own way rather than God's. Isaiah vividly describes it when he says, "all we like sheep have gone astray, we have turned every one to his own way". Our 'way' may not be particularly wicked, but the fact that it is chosen in preference to God's way makes it sinful, and implies a refusal to conform to His will.

The third kind of sins is *'going across'*. The Bible words for this are 'transgression' and 'trespass'. This time the idea is that of crossing a forbidden frontier. It is the most serious side of sin, because it means that we have broken God's laws, and implies not just failure or oversight, but wilful rebellion. All sin by its very nature must separate us from a holy God, but it is because of our transgressions that we provoke "most justly His wrath and indignation against us", and "worthily deserve to be punished".

It is perfectly true that all this is continually stressed in the Bible, but only that it may throw into even stronger and brighter relief the plan of forgiveness which God has worked out for mankind, like the black cloth on which the jeweller places the ring or brooch. And people will only fully appreciate the remedy if they have become convinced of the deadly nature of the disease.

A word finally about 'sin' in the singular. The Bible often refers to this sinful human nature as the 'flesh', and makes it quite clear that we must expect it to remain with us until we die. Just as there is something in steel which makes it respond to magnetic power, so there is within us that which makes it easy and natural for us to do what we know to be wrong, and to respond to the power of temptation. We must not allow this fact to worry us, because it is something which even the best of Christians experience.

But is there anything we can do about it? Yes, there is! Although the tendency to sin cannot be eradicated, it can be counter-balanced. Christ not only died to bring us pardon for our sins, but He also rose again to give us power to overcome sin. His Holy Spirit living within us, provided He is given full control, can neutralize this bias towards evil and give us, not immunity from its presence, but deliverance from its power. We shall be like people suffering from one of those diseases such as diabetes which can never be completely rooted out of the system, but may be permanently and satisfactorily controlled provided we take sensible precautions, have a carefully-balanced diet, and use the necessary drugs.

28 | If God loves us, why could He not forgive us without Christ's having to die for us ?

WE must begin by reminding ourselves that God is absolutely holy and righteous. This means that human sin contradicts His whole way of doing things, and by its very nature is bound to provoke His enmity and opposition. This righteousness is expressed in many places in the Bible, notably in the Ten Commandments, and we have only to test ourselves by these, in the fuller interpretation given to them by Christ, to see how far short we have come of God's standards, and how inevitably we have incurred His wrath.

That is why the Bible tells us that "the wages of sin is death", or separation from God. If a motorist repeatedly and deliberately violates the rules of the road, people agree that his licence or freedom to drive should be taken away from him. In other words, for him "the wages of sin is death", that is, the end of his life as a motorist. In the same way, man has offended against God, and the consequence of his doing so is the end of a life of friendship with Him, and expulsion from His presence for ever.

"But," protests someone, "while I can see all this, have you not left out of account the love of God? I can see that in the normal, human way a man may have to suffer the consequences of his misdeeds, but surely God is infinitely loving, and could have overlooked our sins and forgiven us." Could He? We would have little enough respect for a father or a schoolmaster or a magistrate who waived the rules when he felt like it, and failed to conform to the accepted standards of righteousness and justice. How much less can God behave like that? He must uphold His own standard of moral righteousness; and an immoral God (and that is what He would be) is unthinkable. Better no God at all than one who could condone evil.

But in fact, of course, God's infinite love was shown to us, not in ignoring our sin, but in providing a remedy. It is perfectly true that man is sinful, that sin brings death, and that a holy and righteous God must execute that sentence; but it was precisely at this point that His wonderful love was seen in the gift to mankind of His Son, Jesus Christ, Who died upon the Cross for our redemption.

What happened on the Cross was this: Jesus Christ, God's Son, accepted in Himself the full consequences of man's sin, even enduring the final and awful separation from His Father's presence; and because of this "full, perfect and sufficient sacrifice" God was able to forgive man without in any way violating His own character of holiness. It may help to think of it in this way. The fine imposed had to be paid by man, but it could only be paid by God; therefore God became man that He might accept the responsibility of human sin, bear the burden of His own broken law, and pay from the infinite resources of His love the fine which His justice demanded.

But there is a further problem which perplexes some people, and we must try to deal with it. Was it morally right for God to allow Christ to die in our place like that? After all, no human judge would dream of allowing such an arrangement. The answer lies in the relationship which exists in that 'mysterious Godhead, three in one'. It was not just a question of God's punishing Jesus in our place. The unity between Father and Son was such that Paul could say, "God was in Christ, reconciling the world unto

Himself"; and in some way which we cannot understand, the Father Himself actually shared the suffering, sorrow and desolation of His Son.

Again, it is sometimes asked how the death of one man, two thousand years ago, can deal effectively with the sins of the whole world, and especially with the sins of those people who at that time had never lived. The answer lies in the nature and character of the man who died. Jesus was not just a very good man, He was absolutely without sin; and He was not simply a great prophet and teacher, He was the Son of God Himself. It is these two things, His sinlessness and His deity, which made His sacrifice upon the Cross of such infinite and eternal value to mankind.

29 Isn't it enough to follow the example of Jesus without believing that He is divine?

THERE are many people who think like this. They would call themselves 'Ethical Christians'. They freely admit that nowhere else can we find higher standards than those which are set by Jesus, or wiser teaching, and they simply ask to be allowed to put them into practice in their daily lives. "Why try to build on the foundation of Jesus' life and teaching all this complicated structure of theology and doctrine? Let us get back to the simplicity of Jesus, and try to obey His teaching and copy His example." That is how the argument runs, and people who feel like that would prefer to end their New Testaments with the gospels. "I am all for Jesus," they say, "but I can't take that chap Paul."

Before tackling this problem, I think we ought to say that there is a grain of truth in what is said. It is possible to lose sight of the historical Jesus in the mists of theology. Even the stately language of the Authorized Version tends to obscure the directness and simplicity with which He spoke to and was understood by His hearers. That is one reason why I welcome modern translations like the New English Bible.

But having said that, I think the questioner is really trying to stand things on their head. The implication behind the question is that clever men like Paul have come along and constructed a system of doctrine and then tried to fit it on to Jesus, even twisting the facts of His life to adapt them more suitably to their theories; whereas really what happened was that Paul and John and the others were compelled by the very facts to reach the doctrines which they develop in the later books of the New Testament.

Sometimes you read a book about a person a little casually, and then you see a screen production of that person on TV. At first you are dismayed. "They've got him all wrong," you say, "he's not really a bit like that." Then you have gone back to the book again, and read it more thoughtfully and carefully, and you have realized that the producer has after all understood the person better than you have yourself. You have overlooked certain facets of his character, hints here and suggestions there, which you now begin to see have fully justified the interpretation given on the TV.

Now when we turn to the later writers of the New Testament, our first reaction may be to say, 'They've got Him all wrong'; but if we take the trouble to go back to the gospels, and study them with greater care, we shall begin to see how inescapable is the interpretation of Jesus which they give us—an interpretation, incidentally, which Christians believe was not arrived at through human wisdom, but by the inspiration of the Holy Spirit.

They claim, for example, that Jesus was the Son of God, a completely unique Person. But what else could they say in the light of His supernatural birth, His amazingly authoritative teaching, His miracles of healing, His power over nature, His sinless life, His resurrection, and the conviction which began to grow upon His disciples, even before His departure, that He was divine?

They claim also that His death was not just that of a martyr in a great cause, but that He died sacrificially for the sins of the world, to bring forgiveness to mankind. But what other conclusions could they reach when they considered the emphasis placed upon His death by Jesus Himself? How else are they to understand His frequent references to His sacrifice, the way He identified Himself with the Passover lamb, and His institution of the Holy Communion?

They claim, furthermore, that He will return to this earth, and that He is the man by whom God will judge the world. But what else could they believe in the light of His constant references to this subject? What other interpretation was open to them when dealing with the occasions on which He spoke of His return, and the many parables in which He figured as the holy and righteous Judge?

Surely it is the questioner who has 'got Him all wrong'. If we admit the miraculous and superhuman element in the life of Jesus, then we are driven to accept also the kind of interpretation which Paul and the others give us. If on the other hand we try to distil these elements out of the life of Jesus, then we do hopeless violence to the gospel story, and what we are left with is not even a great historical figure whose example we must follow, but either that of an impostor or a lunatic.

30 | Isn't it enough if I do my best? Won't God accept me because of that?

A T first sight this does seem a very reasonable and attractive idea. Surely if I lead a good and a religious life God will be pleased with me, and forgive my misdeeds. After all, we live in a competitive world, in what has been called a 'meritocracy'. The battle goes to the strong, the race to the swift, the prizes to the intelligent, so why not heaven to the good? Moreover, it might keep everyone on their toes, and make them behave a good deal better, if they thought that their eternal salvation depended upon some kind of examination at the end of their lives, a sort of 80 +.

First of all we must remind ourselves that sin is the breaking of God's law, and carries with it the penalty of separation from His presence. Now it should be obvious that a broken law cannot be repaired by good resolutions for the future. My emphatic promise never to exceed the speed limit again will not persuade the magistrate to let me off the fine I have deserved for exceeding it last week. One of our best known hymns puts this very forcibly when it says, "Not the labour of my hands can fulfil Thy law's demands; could my zeal no respite know, could my tears for ever flow, all for sin could not atone . . ."

In the second place we must realize how very poor our 'best' is The prophet Isaiah said, "All our righteousnesses are as filthy rags". Most of us would be prepared to admit that our sins deserve that sort of description, but surely not our righteousnesses? But the trouble is that sin has become so inextricably woven into our nature, that selfishness and pride often colour and even motivate what look like some of our noblest words and deeds. We may have a fine opinion of ourselves, and we may compare very favourably with other people we know; but in God's sight "there is none righteous, no, not one", and in His pure presence we are rather like unkempt vagabonds who have found their way into the middle of a Buckingham Palace Garden Party.

Thirdly, have you ever thought what an impossible sort of place heaven would be if we were to owe our presence there to our own good deeds, and it could only be entered by merit? No wonder Paul was inspired to write, "By grace are ye saved through faith; and that not of yourselves, *lest any man should boast*". It would be a kind of home for prigs, and I am not sure that I wouldn't be happier somewhere else. But, thank God, heaven is not selective in this sense, but comprehensive, and there will be a place for everyone who accepts the terms of entry.

Lastly, if forgiveness depended upon human merit, what about the many people who have little or no chance of acquiring any? What about the dying thief on the cross? As far as we can see, he turned to Christ, truly repenting, and believing in Him; but he had precious little time left to score any good marks. How would he fare? Surely God's great love is seen partly in the fact that He does not accept us on the grounds of merit, but has provided a way whereby "the vilest offender who truly believes that moment from Jesus a pardon receives". In this way there is an entry, even for those who sincerely turn to Christ at the last moment.

But it is very important that I should end by saying this: Although the good life can never earn our forgiveness, it can and indeed it must express our gratitude to God. We may not be saved *by* good works, but we are unquestionably saved *"unto* good works". And when Paul says that "a man is justified by faith, without (apart from) the deeds of the law", it is perfectly clear that he means the kind of faith which will eventually prove itself in a life that is good and acceptable to God. Later on in the same epistle (to the Romans) he castigates those who were arguing that, because they were now forgiven, they could behave as they liked and continue to sin; and James, in his epistle, goes so far as to say that the faith by which such people claim to have received forgiveness in the first place is empty, dead and meaningless if it allows them to speak like that.

31 | How can I become a Christian ?

S o often we hear sermons or read articles about the Christian life, and what it means to be a Christian. But until we know how to become a Christian, talks on Christian experience can make little or no sense.

Putting it in its simplest terms, there are three steps into the Christian life, three things which we must do if we want to have Christ as our Saviour and Friend.

First, we must *admit our need*. Most people would agree that sin is the thing which more than anything else spoils life. We do not have to be very observant to see that it is man's selfishness and greed which, amongst other things, set nations against each other; while many homes are spoiled by the thoughtlessness, the unkindness, the sulkiness and selfish obstinacy of one or more of their members. In personal life too, the thing which really distresses us, when we are honest with ourselves, is sin. It is that which nags at our conscience, and often gets such a grip upon our wills that we find it impossible to break free.

All this is true, but we must remember that the true sinfulness of sin consists in the fact that it comes between ourselves and God, making friendly relations with Him impossible, and exposing us to His judgment; for the barrier between man and his Maker is not an intellectual one, due to our mental dullness, and failure to understand Him, but a moral one, caused by our disobedience and sin. There can be no reconciliation between man and God so long as he persists in the course resulting from his universal declaration of independence. It may be a very hard and humbling thing to have to do, to admit our need and abandon our sin; but until the patient admits that there is something wrong with his health, he will not send for the doctor; and until a person admits that he is a sinner, in need of forgiveness, he will never turn to Christ.

And the next step is to *believe that Christ died for us*. We have seen the complaint, now we must see the cure. The man who admits that he is sick will make no progress until he hears of and believes in someone who can put him right. It was just that which Jesus came to do. All His life was spent putting right what had gone wrong. He began as a Carpenter, mending the things which people brought to Him. He continued as a Physician, healing their bodies and their minds. Finally, He became a Saviour, curing people's souls, and offering them forgiveness and power.

It was this which led Him to the Cross; for there, outside the ancient city wall, the Lord Jesus Christ offered His life as a sacrifice for the sins of the world. Bearing the burden which should have been ours, accepting the judgment which should have fallen upon us, He "suffered for sins, the just for the unjust, that He might bring us to God". This is the glorious fact we must believe. Jesus did not just die as a martyr in a great cause, nor even as a token of God's unquenchable love; He died that we might be forgiven by taking upon Himself the responsibility and guilt of human sin.

But a third step is necessary. The cure and the complaint, the physician and the patient must be brought together, and that happens when we *commit ourselves to Christ*. Actually, this step is in two parts. First, we must abandon what we know to be wrong. We cannot ask the doctor to treat us if we are determined to continue doing the very things which cause and aggravate our complaint. And we cannot come to Christ for forgiveness, unless first we turn from our sins.

Then we must accept the Saviour, by putting ourselves into His hands, and becoming His patients, His pupils. The New Testament has many different word-pictures which describe this final step. It speaks of 'coming to Christ', of 'receiving Him' and of 'trusting Him'. They are all illustrations of the same thing, namely a wholehearted committal of ourselves to Him, and a determination to be His faithful soldiers and servants unto our lives' end.

We shall soon find that we have far to go and much to learn, but this is how it all begins.

32 | How can I know whether I am a Christian or not ?

FIRST of all, I would say this: "Have you ever consciously and deliberately become a Christian? Have you come to see your need of Christ, and put your trust in Him as your

Saviour and Friend?" This need not be a sudden or dramatic experience, but unless there has been that beginning, I am afraid most of what follows will not make sense. We cannot begin to know that we are alive until we have been born; or that we are in a new country until we have crossed the frontier.

"Yes," you say, "I have done that, but how do I know that I did it properly?" Don't worry about that! If, as best you knew how, you responded to the call of Christ, then you can be sure that all is well. It is not the exact form of words that matters, but the attitude of your heart and mind. No sensible man will worry himself sick over whether or not he used the right formula when proposing marriage to the girl he loved. He may even have put it as gloomily as the man who said, "Would you like to have my name on your tombstone?" But what does it matter? If they are happily married, that is all that counts.

Perhaps, like me, you can look back upon an actual day when it all began. I think it is helpful if we can, though not necessary. The Children of Israel used to be encouraged to raise a cairn of stones to mark some historic event in their journeyings, and I can still remember that Sunday evening, in the August of 1932, when, after a period of searching and uncertainty, I started my Christian pilgrimage.

However that may be, it is important for our own peace of mind and for our usefulness in Christian service to be able to say, "I know", and not simply "I hope so", or "I think so", when someone asks us if we are a Christian. How can we be certain? In two ways—by faith and by experience.

First, we must believe the promises of Christ. If we have come to Him, then He will in no wise cast us out; if we have received Him, then we can be certain that He has come in. If I were to ask you how you knew that you had passed your driving test, paid that bill, been chosen for that team, got that place at the university, or for that matter were a member of the Brown or Robinson family, what would your answer be? You would simply find the appropriate letter, list, receipt or certificate, and you would say,

"Look it says so here." And that would end the argument.

Now the part played by those written assurances in ordinary life is much the same as the part played by the written promises of God. We must hold on to them, treasure them and believe them. There may be times when we do not feel that they are true, or are tempted to doubt them. No matter; God cannot deny Himself, and so, calmly and cold-bloodedly, we must take Him at His word. His promises are our final authority for saying that we are Christians, and members of His family.

But although you will never discard those written promises, there will come a time when you will no longer need to rely upon them quite so exclusively, because if you really are a Christian, then sooner or later you will begin to know it in your own experience. If I say to one of you who is married, "How do you know that you are married to so-and-so?" What would you say? Would you look at your watch and say, "We've just time to get to Somerset House before it closes, come with me, and I will show you the marriage certificate"? Surely not! You would produce a photograph of your children, and say, "Look, here are my children, the fruit of my marriage". Or you would show me a silver pencil, and say, "This is what my wife (or husband) gave me for Christmas". In a hundred and one ways you would prove to me from your own experience that you were in fact married to the person concerned.

Now the part played by those signs in ordinary life is much the same as the part played by the Holy Spirit in your Christian experience. He will begin to implant within you new desires. You will begin to find, gradually and increasingly, that you hate what is sinful and love what is good. You will find that the Bible becomes a new book to you, and that prayer begins to mean something positive and helpful. You will find that you enjoy the company of other Christian people, and that, in Wesley's words, your heart is 'strangely warmed' towards Christ Himself.

33 | How can I get rid of my doubts?

IT could be said that we live in an age of doubt. In the last hundred years cherished beliefs and traditions have been challenged as never before. From every angle these attacks have come—psychological, moral, scientific and historical. Nothing is immune. Nothing is sacred. Besides living in an age of doubt, many of us are probably living at an age of doubt. As a child we took everything for granted. The questions that interested us were, 'When?' 'Where?' 'What?' And we were content to take the answers pretty well on trust. But very soon our critical and analytical faculties began to develop, and we were encouraged to ask a whole lot of new questions—'Whether?' 'Why?' 'How?' Indeed, the whole art of education is to examine subjects like science, history and literature in this ruthless and vigorous way. But is religion to be exempt? Are we to withdraw our intellectual antennae as we approach its sacred frontiers? Surely the answer must be 'No'! At some stage we should all want to know whether Christianity can stand on its own feet, or is one huge confidence trick.

This is not the moment to embark upon an elaborate defence of the Christian Faith, but what I can do here is to indicate the lines along which doubts can be answered. The first is the authority of Christ Himself. The acceptability of any statement depends not so much upon the credibility of that statement itself as upon the reliability of the person who makes it. For instance, what seems to be the most unlikely rumour may get abroad, but if you can convince yourself that the source from which it springs is absolutely unimpeachable, then you feel yourself bound to say, "Well, it simply *must* be true". Now in the case of Christ, we either have to admit that He was a conscious and deliberate fraud,

78

or that He was self-deceived to the point of lunacy, or that what He said about Himself was true. No other choice is open to us. And as I read His life, I feel myself compelled to believe that He was all that He professed to be.

Secondly, there is the testimony of the Church. Despite its divisions and its failures, it has always fortified me to know that Christians of all churches, all down the ages, including the 230 million or so who are alive today, subscribe to the same basic beliefs of the Christian religion, namely the existence of God and the divinity of Christ. I personally find myself upheld by the thought that so many wise men have held these beliefs, so many good men have been guided by them, and so many brave men have suffered imprisonment and death rather than be parted from them.

Thirdly, I derive great confidence from the effects of the Gospel throughout the world. Again and again it has shown its power to change individual lives and to inspire social reform. When John the Baptist, riddled with doubt, sent his message to Jesus, "Art Thou He that should come, or look we for another?" Jesus did not give him the direct answer, "Yes" or "No". Instead, He said, "Go and tell John what things you have seen and heard. . . ." And I believe the answer is still the same. It is there, in mended lives and transformed characters, that we find the strongest evidence for the claims of Christianity.

It is these three things which have helped me in time of doubt. Of course they do not constitute a complete answer, but only the opening moves of a defence. Indeed, we shall never completely dispel doubt, for if it were impossible to doubt, how could we believe? We would simply be forced into an intellectual assent from which there would be no escape. Cast-iron certainty would leave no room for faith. Just as a man's reach will always exceed his grasp, so we shall always need faith to carry us, not against reason, but beyond the best that reason can do. And it is worth remembering also that the unbeliever has only exchanged one kind of doubt for another.

Finally, face your doubts squarely, and don't pretend they

are not there; tackle them sensibly, with careful thought and study; and, most important of all, regard them suspiciously!

34 | Why are so many non-Christians much nicer than Christians?

I AM reminded of the small girl who was heard to pray, "Please God, make all the nice people good, and the good people nice." But before we accept the implication of her prayer, and of this question, I think we must be quite clear what we mean by this word 'nice'. If a 'nice' person is one who possesses the basic qualities of kindheartedness, generosity, humility and integrity, then I don't think that either the little girl or the questioner is right. I believe those qualities are more often seen in Christians than in non-Christians, and if I were in any sort of trouble, it is to a Christian that I would turn for comfort and counsel.

But if the word 'nice' is meant to suggest the more superficial qualities of charm, affability and friendliness, then I think there is something in the criticism; for very often these things are missing in the Christian, and I have often wondered why. Any who have read Sir Edmund Gosse's book *Father and Son* will agree that, virtuous and upright though the father was, they would infinitely have preferred to play a round of golf with the friendly, agnostic son. I am afraid that it is true that there is too often a streak of hardness, inflexibility and censoriousness about Christian people which is very unattractive. They are quick to criticize and find fault, focusing their attention more readily on the black squares of the chess-board than on the white.

Without making excuses it is, I think, possible to explain why non-Christians often appear more attractive than Christians, just as some artificial flowers are nicer to look at than those you pick in the garden. Sometimes, in their pursuit of the basic and important virtues, Christians are apt to overlook, and even perhaps to suspect and eschew the more obvious and superficial graces of life. Up to a point they are right. There is something deceptive about outward charm. If I had to paint a modern portrait of the Devil, he would be the most engaging, sociable and charming person you could imagine, with nothing coarse or savage about him. He would, of course, have that more brutish side to his character, but more often than not it would be coated with the most agreeable friendliness.

Christian people are therefore perhaps wise to be a little on their guard where worldly charm is concerned, but having said that, there ought, I am sure, to be a kind of Christian pleasantness of manner and behaviour which is even more attractive. Paul's famous chapter on love is really saying this when he touches on patience, modesty, courtesy and good manners; and these things ought to be apparent in those who follow Christ, as well as the more fundamental virtues.

Here, as in so many other things, the perfect example is to be found in Christ Himself. It is said that He was 'full of grace and truth'. That is the balance which His followers must seek to achieve. We must be full of 'truth', ready to stand for all that is right and good, and prepared never to condone evil, even at the cost of making ourselves socially unpopular. What is black we must call black, and not try to pretend that it is simply grey or off-white. But at the same time we must be full of 'grace', holding 'the truth in love'. If we have this love for our fellow-men, sharing, that is, the love which Christ has towards them, then His beauty and graciousness will be seen in our lives.

There must have been something wonderfully attractive about Jesus. Little children came to Him, publicans and sinners enjoyed His company, intellectuals like Nicodemus went out of their way to meet Him, and yet immoral women somehow felt that He did not regard them as 'beyond the pale'. Winsome, attractive, sympathetic, yes; and yet I doubt whether we would have called Him 'nice' in the superficial sense of that word. He could be disturbingly frank. We can imagine that when He came into the room the unkind remark was somehow checked, the oath bitten back at the last moment, the lie shrivelled up on the speaker's tongue, and the dirty story went untold. I am sure that is true; but I am equally sure that the next moment these same people were laughing with Him, confiding in Him, and jostling with each other to get as close to Him as they could. If only all Christians were like their Master, they would perhaps be good *and* nice; but there would be a quality about their niceness which no one would dream of calling hollow or superficial.

35 | Why have so many of the greatest people not been Christians?

I THINK probably this point has to be conceded, but I don't think it need surprise us unduly, because it is no new discovery. In fact it is precisely what Paul found. "My brothers," he said, "think what sort of people you are, whom God has called. Few of you are men of wisdom by any human standard; few are powerful or highly born." (N.E.B.) But he goes on to tell them not to worry, because their poverty and obscurity provide God with a greater opportunity for exercising His power and enhancing His glory.

It is only fair to add that there are many notable exceptions to this rule, and a large number of very great men and women, as the world itself judges greatness, have accepted the Christian Faith all down the ages; while others who might have become great have been willing to lose themselves in the service of Christ. But the fact remains that the Gospel has always made most effective headway amongst simple and lowly people, and it would be well therefore to analyse what we mean by greatness, and see why it does so often seem to present such a stumbling-block to acceptance of the Christian Faith.

First, there are those with a *great brain*. They are so used to seeking proofs for what they believe, that the idea of trusting in Christ for salvation seems altogether too simple and naive to their way of thinking. Jesus warned us that this would be so when He said that these things were hidden from the wise and prudent, and revealed unto babes. It is not easy to convince the very clever man that spiritual truth is not understood by a mental process, or that it can be conveyed to him along any other level than that of the intellect; and perhaps that is why we often find amongst Christians a simple and even a stupid man who has a far clearer grasp of Christian truth, and much greater facility in expressing it, than an intelligent one.

Secondly, there are those who enjoy *great power*. Here I think the stumbling-block is not so much doubt as pride. It is very hard for a man who is in a position of considerable authority to humble himself sufficiently to submit to the sovereignty of Christ. Power tends to corrupt those who exercise it, and even in a small way it can be a hindrance. The captain of the team is going to find it just that much harder to become an ordinary member of Christ's family. The director needs to be very humble if he is going to become one of Christ's servants or employees, and the general too, if he is to be a private soldier in the army of Christ.

Thirdly, there are those who achieve *great fame*. In the old days this would probably have been on the field of battle, or in politics. It can still be so; but the sporting and entertainment worlds have opened to a far wider circle of people a short-cut to the headlines, and at a much earlier age. Here I believe the snare is fear—fear of man. It needs a lot of courage, for example, for a TV personality to let it be known that he is a Christian, or for a famous footballer to risk the mockery of his friends by coming out on Christ's side. So many people will hear, talk or laugh about it, that all too frequently he dare not face the challenge, and remains at best a secret disciple of Christ.

Fourthly, there are those who have *great wealth*. This time the danger is perhaps the strongest of all—love: love of money. Money is like a drug. It has two effects. First, it produces a false sense of security and well-being, because it paves the way to very desirable but temporal things like comfort, leisure and luxury; and secondly, at the same time, it masks the symptoms of our fundamental need of Christ as Saviour and Friend. Perhaps more than anything else, money, with all that it can obtain for us, keeps people from Christ. Think of the 'Rich Young Ruler', and of what Jesus said to him.

All this adds up to the fact that for the great people of the world the cost of discipleship is often very much more severe than it is for the simple and the ordinary, and therefore perhaps it is only to be expected that fewer of them are found in the ranks of Christians. But we must be careful to add that when a great man turns to Christ, it is wonderful how his gifts can be used; for his mind, power, fame and wealth can be harnessed to the service of God and the promotion of His glory. Does not the apostle Paul himself provide us with a supreme example of this truth?

36 | Doesn't the idea of being thought 'religious' put many people off?

I THINK it probably does. The trouble is that the word 'religion' has become devalued, and is more often associated with the outward forms and trappings of Christianity than with its inward spirit. In the minds of some it suggests long, rambling sermons, unintelligible prayers, and people who look as if they are always on their way to or from a funeral. This is a pity, because in its original sense the word is a fine one. It comes from the Latin *religare*, meaning 'to tie back', and describes the bond which exists between man and God, and the effect this relationship should have upon his everyday life.

We must of course be careful not to use the word as if it were an alternative to Christianity. Many people do. They speak of someone as being 'religious' when what they mean is 'Christian'. But there are many religions in the world, and you can be religious without being in the least bit Christian, just as you can be British without having a drop of Welsh or even English blood in your veins. But the converse is not true. You cannot be Welsh or English without being British, and you cannot be a Christian without being religious.

When we look into the matter more closely, we find in fact that all the great religions of the world, Christianity, Buddhism, Hinduism and the rest, have certain things in common with each other. There is, first of all, a belief in the existence of some sort of superhuman being. They differ sharply in what they believe about His character and attributes. At one extreme are those who think of Him as a remote and distant figure who once set the world going, and now stands back to watch it like a model railway, even leaving it to its fate. This idea is usually called 'Deism'. At the opposite end of the spectrum is 'Pantheism', in which God is identified with His universe and inseparable from it. But however unsatisfactory ideas like these may be from the Christian point of view, they do stand for something, and a religious man, asked whether he believes in God, will unhesitatingly say, "Yes".

The second factor common to all religions is that in some way this God is entitled to our homage, respect and worship. As far as I know, there is no religion which has not developed some system of worship. It may be very debased and primitive, but at least it represents an attempt on the part of man to get in touch with God, to reverence Him and to show His 'worth-ship', which is the idea behind the word 'worship'. Sometimes we say of someone that football, or music, is his 'religion'. We mean that these are the things which he values and loves most. They hold first place in his heart and mind. They are the object of his worship. Money is another example, and Bernard Shaw

made one of his characters say, "I am a Millionaire. That
is my religion."

The third thing which most religions have in common is
a standard of behaviour, or to use theological jargon, a
code of ethics. A religious man, whatever his religion may
be, will nearly always allow it to influence the way he
lives. However imperfectly, his faith will be translated into
action; and because he feels that he is directly accountable
to the God he worships, his conduct will usually be of a
higher standard than that of a man who professes no
religion at all.

What we have said so far leaves deliberately untouched
the question of which religion is the right one. The word
'religion', as we have seen, is completely neutral. If, for
example, I have to try to define what a politician is, I don't
say 'a Socialist, a Conservative or a Liberal'. I say that a
politician is someone who holds certain strong political
beliefs, who pledges his allegiance to the party which shares
those beliefs, and who does his best to put them into practice. For all I know he may have political opinions which
I abhor, but that does not alter the fact that he has every
right to be called a politician.

In the same way we might say that a religious man is one
who is bound to God by the threefold cord of confidence,
reverence and obedience; and this is the true value which
we want to restore to a much maligned and misused word.
Applied in this sense to the Christian it certainly ought
not to cause him any feeling of embarrassment or shame.

37 | Do you believe in sudden conversion ? Surely it takes a lifetime to become a Christian ?

I THINK we had better begin by becoming quite clear what
we mean by 'conversion'. It is not just a decision to follow Christ, made as the result of a stirring appeal or a

powerful sermon. It is not simply an intellectual conviction about the divinity of Christ. True conversion, we may say, affects a man at four levels—in his mind, his conscience, his heart and his will. First, he must understand Who Christ is and what He has done; secondly, he must realize his own sinfulness, and his need of a Saviour and Keeper; thirdly, he must have in his heart a desire to follow Christ which springs, however feebly, from a love for One Who has done so much for him; and fourthly and finally, he must respond to the call of Christ, coming to Him, and opening to Him the door of his heart and life.

Conversion is therefore a tremendous thing. It affects the whole of the personality. It is possible to have an 'experience' along any one of the four levels I have indicated —to be intellectually convinced, or perhaps emotionally stirred; but true conversion is a 'vertical' and not a 'horizontal' experience, involving every level of the personality, and I doubt whether we can really call a person a Christian, or say that he is converted, unless he can say four things, "I see; I ought; I want; I will."

In the light of this, do I believe in sudden conversion? I am perfectly sure that conversion is both sudden and gradual, but that it is never as sudden on the one hand, or as gradual on the other as some people would have us believe. The most dramatic conversion in history was surely that of St Paul, and yet it is evident that for some time his conscience had been at work, that his defences were being undermined, and that what happened on the road to Damascus was simply the final and total collapse of his resistance. On the other hand, his experience teaches us that there must in fact be a point in time when the frontier is reached and crossed, however slowly we approach it, and however long we linger in its vicinity.

Two analogies may help us. The Bible compares becoming a Christian to awakening out of sleep. Now we all know there are two ways of waking up. We can wake up gradually, as the rising sun steals through the windows, and brings an almost imperceptible return to consciousness.

Or we can wake up with a start, as the bugle sounds, or the alarm clock rings, or when we hear someone knocking at the door, or calling us down to breakfast. In both cases the frontier of consciousness had to be approached and crossed, but it could not matter less how and when my sleep ended, so long as I know that I am now 'awake to righteousness'.

Conversion is also compared to the new birth, and here again we have an experience which is both sudden and gradual. We speak, for example, of a 'birthday', and not a 'birthweek' or a 'birthmonth', thus admitting that it is something which happens suddenly, and yet at the same time every birth is but the climax of a long-drawn-out process. But once again the important thing is not to be able to remember when or where we were born, but to know that we are 'alive unto God'.

I come now to the second part of the question where I detect considerable confusion of thought. We must distinguish carefully between our status and our state. If, for example, I am a Frenchman who is about to become a naturalized Englishman, there is a moment in time when my status is officially changed, and from that moment onwards I am an Englishman. But although I am an Englishman, my state of mind is still very French, and it takes me a long time to lose my continental accent, to adopt the customs and habits of my new country and to become English; to become in character what I am in fact.

In his letter to the Romans, Paul makes a very clear distinction between being justified and being sanctified; that is, between being reckoned right in a legal sense and made right in a moral one. The first is a crisis, and can take place in a moment of time; the second is a process which lasts a lifetime. I can become a Christian in an hour, but it will take me all my life to become Christ-like. Birth may be a crisis, over in a few minutes; but growth is a process which will go on for ever, as day by day, year by year, through prayer and Bible reading, Christian worship and fellowship, I get spiritually stronger and stronger.

38 | If God knows everything we need, then what is the point of prayer?

It is important to say at the outset that God does give us many things without our asking for them at all. Probably the vast majority of our daily needs are met without prayer or even thought on our part. Think of the clothing, the food, the shelter, the health which you have enjoyed today. Did you ask for these things last night? I doubt it; but God in His goodness, 'daily loadeth us with benefits.' He, the perfect Father, knows our needs before we ask.

But if there are things which, in His great wisdom, God has decided only to give us in answer to prayer, then that in itself ought to be sufficient reason for us to pray. We know that prayer cannot be a way of informing God about something He does not know already, or reminding Him of something He has forgotten; but if He has attached a condition to giving us what we need, and that condition is that we should ask for those things in prayer, then, whatever we may feel about the logic of it, we ought certainly to pray.

But is there no logic in it? I think there is. God is dealing with us as with children, and to ask a human father for things which we need, and which we know that only he can provide, is the most natural and sensible way in the world of doing two things. First, it is the obvious way of *expressing our desire*. Even the simplest request at the breakfast table, like "Please will you pass the marmalade," shows that we have reached the stage of the meal when marmalade is what we want more than anything else, and that if the request is granted, it won't be wasted on us. It would be unnatural if the desires in our hearts never found expression on our lips.

Secondly, prayer is a way of *expressing our dependence*

upon God, and indeed of increasing it. Even the request for the marmalade showed that in a trivial way. Perhaps we could not reach it ourselves, or someone else was using it at the time, and so, by asking for it, we showed our dependence upon that person to supply what we needed. Prayer is our way of doing that with God. We say, in effect, "I need this courage or wisdom; God alone can supply it; therefore I depend upon Him to do so."

I wonder whether we can now begin to see why it is that very often we do not get what we ask for straightaway. It is not that God does not want us to have it, but He wants to test the reality of our desire and of our dependence upon Himself. You may remember that there was a woman once who came to Jesus, asking Him to heal her daughter; but Jesus 'answered her not a word'. Why this unusual, uncharacteristic silence? I believe He was putting her to the test. Did she really want this thing? Did she really believe He could work this miracle? How triumphantly she passed the test! Her persistence was rewarded, and perhaps the lack of this splendid quality is the reason why more of our prayers are not granted.

Of course, we must remember that, in His Father-like wisdom, God often has to say "No". Like ordinary children, it is all too easy for us to ask for things at the wrong time, or in the wrong way, or for the wrong reason, and when this happens, our requests have to be postponed and even refused. But usually, if we live close to God, we come to see the reason for this, and to realize that our prayers have in fact been answered, even though our petitions have not been granted.

There is, I think, another aspect of this subject (particularly where praying for others is concerned), which ought to be touched upon. We know that prayer cannot change God's mind, but the Bible does seem to suggest that there is a way in which it can set His hands free to work. It speaks about 'striving' or 'wrestling' in prayer, and it would appear from this that prayer is a power which can be used to restrain and to defeat the Satanic forces of evil which are operating in the world. We do not know exactly how this works, but there seems to be no doubt that prayer is the Christian's 'secret weapon', and that by using it we are in fact helping God, even when we are asking Him to help us. Indeed, prayer is a way of enabling God to get His will done on earth, just as it is in heaven. It is obvious that this adds greatly to the importance of prayer, and may also explain why sometimes it is so difficult.

39 If God wants us to be good, why does He allow us to be tempted?

BASICALLY, this question has got a flaw in it. In fact it should not be a question at all, 'If God wants us to be good, why does He allow us to be tempted?', but rather a statement, 'Because God wants us to be good, He allows us to be tempted'. In other words, we cannot be good unless we are tempted and put to the test, because goodness is not untried innocence, but victorious virtue. Suppose your school or college has a cricket eleven which looks on paper to be one of the best ever, but for some reason, illness, perhaps, or bad weather, it is able to play no matches throughout the season. You cannot describe it as a 'good' team. You can call it promising, full of potential, very experienced, if you like; but you cannot fairly call it good, because it has never been tested, and you cannot be sure how it would have fared if it had been.

Now temptation is one of God's principal ways of testing us. It reveals what stuff we are made of spiritually, and what our true character is like. It shows how far His teaching has sunk into our hearts, how anxious we are to please Him, and how far we have learnt to rely upon His strength for victory. But the purpose of an examination, as we know, is not only to discover what we know, but also to qualify

us for the next stage in our education or career. And so
the value of temptation lies not only in what it reveals
about our past progress, but also in the way it prepares us
for the future. First, it strengthens our spiritual muscles,
making victory the next time just that much more likely;
and secondly, it teaches us a deeper reliance upon God.

This is why the Bible tells us not only that temptation
itself is not sin, but also that we must consider ourselves
fortunate to be tempted. James actually goes so far as to
say, "Count it all joy when ye fall into divers temptations".
He does not mean that the actual experience of temptation
is a pleasure to be sought for its own sake; but he knew
that after each temptation successfully withstood, the Christian is a little stronger than he was before, a little closer to
God, a little readier for the next battle, and a little more
likely to be useful to his Master.

Of course this question poses a much larger one. It is
easy to see personal and practical reasons why temptation
serves a useful purpose, and that we are likely to become
better characters by having to face it than we would be if
we could avoid it altogether; but how does this satisfy God?
After all, if sin is the thing He hates most of all, then why
did He deliberately make us in such a way that we would
be liable to succumb to it?

We are bound to ask what alternative He had. There
were only two ways in which He could have made man—
either with a free will or without. But if He had made us
like automata, or puppets on a string, conforming in-
voluntarily to His will, would that really have satisfied His
creative instinct? Would not even a human father prefer
to take the risk of launching his son or daughter on the
sea of life rather than keeping them sheltered and cooped
up at home, protected from all the winds of social and
worldly influence? It seems as though God, faced, if we
may say so, with the same sort of choice, made the same
decision. He could have created us so that we were 'not
able to sin'; but instead, He made us 'able not to sin'.

"Yes," says someone, "but your analogy about the human

father is false. He takes the risk, hoping for the best, but God took it knowing the worst; for He must have known that perhaps the vast majority of His creatures would turn from Him and go their own way." I know! But we must believe, despite all that can be argued to the contrary, that somehow in His eternal and infinite view of things, it is more honouring to Him, more in keeping with His character as an almighty and all-loving Creator, to have it this way. It was Samuel Butler who first said, " 'Tis better to have loved and lost, than never to have lost at all." And I wonder sometimes whether there is not something there which applies even to God Himself. Better for man to be given free will, to be tempted, to fall and to be estranged, and then to have the offer of eternal redemption, even though some refuse it: better all that than for God to have created not men, but toys. I wonder!

40 | Isn't it all too simple?

I KNOW what the questioner means. He is told that by 'coming to Christ' or by 'receiving' or 'trusting Him' he can have forgiveness and eternal life. It seems incredible to him that so much can turn upon so little. Can it really be as simple as that? Isn't it just a little too good to be true?

I think my first answer is that it has got to be simple, because 95 per cent of the people in the world are simple people, and if their salvation depended, let us say, on solving some complicated theological crossword puzzle, how many of them would benefit from it? And after all, you don't have to understand all about electricity before you can enjoy the advantages of electric light.

But the question is a little deceptive, because although the actual step of becoming a Christian is simple, it is

neither cheap nor easy. A great deal has led up to it, and a
great deal will stem from it. What could be simpler than
signing your name? It is something which many of us do
dozens of times each week. And yet if you happened to be
a great financier, you could be signing away a fortune; or
if you were a minister of state, you could be signing a great
trade agreement, or a declaration of war. Why, Abraham
Lincoln once spent the whole night pacing up and down
in his room before he could bring himself to put his signa-
ture to some fateful document!

While therefore the act of becoming a Christian, of committing ourselves to Christ, is and must be simple, think
first of what it cost Him to make it so. It is a simple matter
in these days to sail through the Panama Canal, or to motor
across the Firth of Forth; but the canal and the bridge both
cost vast sums of money to build, and also the sacrifice of
some lives. The simplicity which people can now enjoy has
only been made possible by the sacrifice of others. So it is
with the Christian life. The way back to God, the bridge
into the Kingdom of Heaven, is so simple that a child can
take it; but it owes that simplicity to the fact that it re-
quired the death of God's Son to 'unlock the gate'.

Think in the second place of what it will cost us. It may
be a simple matter to cross a frontier, and sometimes we do
it without even knowing; but what a lot that simple step
can involve! It may mean abandoning a way of life we have
known for years; breaking with friends we have had all our
lives; accepting new standards, customs and values.

When slavery was still legal in the United States, but not
in Canada, a man had only to cross the border to be free.
One step, and the shackles fell off for ever! But it was not
as easy as that. There were roots to be dug up and risks to
be run; and it cannot have been the sort of step which any
one took lightly, or without a great deal of heart-searching.

And no one will commit himself to Christ without much
careful thought. Sometimes we meet people who are thinking of emigrating, attracted by the new opportunities over-
seas. Perhaps the most important question they have to con-

sider is the cost of living in Canada or Australia, for example, compared with England. That is what every would-be disciple of Jesus must carefully consider, and you remember how often He reminded those who applied for visas to enter His kingdom to expect a hard, tough life.

Sometimes there is a hint of pride in this question, as though to suggest that if my forgiveness depended upon something I could do myself, it would be more worth having. I am reminded of Naaman. This great general, the darling of his people, discovered to his horror that he had contracted leprosy. Hearing of a man who could work remarkable cures, named Elisha, he set off to see him, laden with gifts. To his dismay, all that the prophet did was to send a message telling him to go and dip himself seven times in the River Jordan. It was an outrageous insult and he 'went away in a rage'; but, happily, he had some good friends, and one of them said to him, "Look here, Sir, if the prophet had told you to do something big, wouldn't you have done it? If he had told you to invade Egypt, or attack Assyria, you would have been off like a shot. How much more, then, when he simply tells you to wash and be clean?" The shaft went home. The great general pocketed his pride, and humbled himself to do something very simple indeed. But was it easy, do you think? And was it cheap?